KU-081-963

The Organizational Learning Cycle

How We Can Learn Collectively

NANCY M. DIXON

McGraw-Hill Book Company

London · New York · St Louis · San Francisco · Auckland
Bogotá · Caracas · Lisbon · Madrid · Mexico
Milan · Montreal · New Delhi · Panama · Paris · San Juan
São Paulo · Singapore · Sydney · Tokyo · Toronto

Published by
McGRAW-HILL Book Company Europe
Shoppenhangers Road, Maidenhead, Berkshire, SL6 2QL, England
Telephone 01628 23432
Fax 01628 770224

British Library Cataloguing in Publication Data

Dixon, Nancy
    Organizational Learning Cycle: How We Can Learn Collectively. –
(McGraw-Hill
    Developing Organizations (Series)   I. Title II. Series
    658.3124

    ISBN 0–07–707937–X

Library of Congress Cataloging-in-Publication Data

    The organizational learning cycle: how we can learn collectively / Nancy
M. Dixon.
    p.   cm.
    Includes bibliographical references and index.
    ISBN 0–07–707937–X:
    1. Communication in organizations. 2. Organizational behavior. 3.
Organizational effectiveness. I. Title.
HD30.3.D58   1994
158.7–dc20   94–17076
                                                                 CIP

Copyright © 1994 McGraw-Hill International (UK) Ltd. All rights
reserved. No part of this publication may be reproduced, stored in a
retrieval system, or transmitted, in any form or by any means, electronic,
mechanical, photocoyping, recording, or otherwise, without the prior
permission of McGraw-Hill International (UK) Ltd.

34 CUP 9765

Typeset by Computape (Pickering) Ltd, North Yorkshire
and printed and bound in Great Britain at the University Press, Cambridge

Printed on permanent paper in compliance with ISO Standard 9706

This book is dedicated to Reg Revans whose thinking has been so far ahead of his time, that after 50 years, the world is only just catching up.

Contents

Series Preface

The McGraw-Hill *Developing Organizations* series is for people in the business of changing, developing and transforming their organizations. The books in the series bring together ideas and practice in the emerging field of organizational learning and development. Bridging theory and action, they contain new ideas, methods and models of how to get things done.

Organizational learning and development is the child of the organization development (OD) movement of the 1960s and 1970s. Then people like Schein, Beckhard, Bennis, Walton, Blake and Mouton defined a *change technology* which was exciting and revolutionary. Now the world has moved on.

The word 'technology' goes with the organization-as-machine metaphor. OD emphasized the *outside-in* application of 'behavioural science' which seems naïve in the context of the power-broking, influence and leverage of today's language. Our dominant metaphor of organizations as organisms or collective living beings requires a balancing *inside-out* focus of development and transformation of what is already there.

Learning is the key to our current dilemmas. We are not just talking about change. Learning starts with you and me, with the person – and spreads to others – if we can organize in ways which encourage it.

Learning is at a premium because we are not so much masters of change as beset by it. There is no single formula or image for the excellent company. Even the idea of 'progress' is problematic, as companies stick to the knitting and go to the wall. Multiple possible futures, the need for discontinuity almost for the sake of it, means that we must be able to think imaginatively, to be able to develop ourselves and, in generative relationships with others, to continually organize and reorganize ourselves.

Organizations are unique, with distinctive biographies, strengths and opportunities. Each creates its own future and finds its own development paths. The purpose of these books is not to offer ready-made tools, but to help you create your own tools from the best new ideas and practices around.

The authors in the series have been picked because they have something to say. You will find in all of the books the personal voice of the writer, and this reflects the voice which each of us needs in our own organizations to do the best we can.

I first met Nancy Dixon some seven or eight years ago when she came to England to visit Reg Revans and research action learning. Already a student of Argyris' Action Science, she was enthusiastic, committed and excited about this way of teaching and learning and was trying it out on her Doctoral Programme for Human Resources specialists at George Washington University. As well as being a pleasure to talk to, I remember being pleased at this living proof that ideas can cross the Atlantic in an East-West direction!

Since then I have worked with Nancy both in the USA and the UK. She contributed two chapters to Action Learning in Practice *on experiences at General Motors and Digital in the USA. She has also contributed to the Learning Company Conferences in the UK presenting some of the material that you can now read in this book. It's very good to have Nancy in this series.*

Mike Pedler

Preface

In writing this book, I have drawn heavily on the literature of organizational learning, much of which has been in existence for twenty years, and in some cases even longer. I also draw on recent concepts from the fields of social cognition and adult development, as well as understandings from organizational and cognitive psychology. These ideas are framed within my own concept of organizational learning.

There are two theorists who have so profoundly influenced my own thinking that I am no longer able to distinguish my ideas from theirs: Reg Revans and Chris Argyris. Fifty years ago, Revans developed the original ideas of action learning. His fundamental belief that 'there is no learning without action and no responsible action without learning' has influenced my writing, my interventions with organizations and my university teaching. The basic values of Argyris, which are valid information, free and informed choice, and vigilant monitoring of the implementation of those choices, have influenced my work with organizations, the way I conduct research, and most significantly how I regard basic human interaction. I have attempted to give credit to both of these theorists when I draw directly upon their writing, but I recognize that their influence colours much of what I have written here in ways I may not even be aware of. Their influence is clearly evidenced in the four major themes of the book:

1. Learning is a part of work and work involves learning; these are not separate functions but intertwined; the separation we have made of them is artificial and often does not serve us well.
2. Learning is not only or even primarily about obtaining correct information or answers from knowledgeable others; it is fundamentally about making meaning out of the experience we and others have in the world.

3. Organizational learning results from intentional and planned efforts to learn. Although it can and does occur accidentally, organizations cannot afford to rely on learning through chance.
4. As a collective we are capable of learning our way to the answers we need to address our difficult problems. It is ourselves we must rely on for these answers rather than experts, who can, at best, only provide us with answers that have worked in the past.

I view organizations as purposeful social systems which have three interrelated tasks: (1) the development of the organization itself, (2) the development of the individuals who comprise the organization, and (3) the development of the larger system of which the organization is a part, the community, nation, and planet (Ackoff, 1981). I have undertaken this book because I have an abiding belief in the power of collective learning to address these three tasks with far greater success than they have previously been addressed.

It is the first of these three tasks which organizations have taken as their primary focus: trying to make the organization more productive and competitive. We have only recently come to comprehend the nested nature of systems well enough to consider that the development of the organization cannot be divorced from the development of those who comprise its sub-systems and the supra-systems in which it is embedded.

In maintaining this unitary and limited focus, we have slighted the development of individuals and remained unresponsive to the common good. When we have attended to these, we have treated them as 'in service of' rather than 'in relationship to' the organization. We have, for example, concerned ourselves with the development of individuals only to the extent that development will make the organization more productive. We have focused on the larger system only to the extent that we are required to legally or that is necessary in order to ward off negative publicity.

Even the efforts we have expended on the first of these tasks, as considerable as they have been, have had little to do with development. Our efforts have often seemed more like persuasion or even at times manipulation. We seem to equate development with trying to make the organization comply with our latest theory. So clumsy are our efforts that, by analogy, if the organization were a budding flower, our development effort would equate to tugging and pulling at the petals with the intent of forcing its growth. We have made little use of the collective reasoning and intelligence of the organization in this development effort. But the collective is capable of changing itself into something new and choiceful if we use learning rather than intimidation as the mechanism for development.

In this book I am trying to clarify organizational learning well enough to assist organizations in developing in ways that do service to and are interrelated with the other two systems. The term development is familiar from its use in 'management development' and 'employee development', programs which strive to develop skills and competencies that are useful in carrying out the organization's strategy. I am, however, using the term in the much fuller sense of the development of the human being. Organizations have put considerable resources into management development, but it is human development that I fear we have badly slighted.

Human development does not stop at the beginning of adulthood; it continues throughout the lifetime of the individual. As human beings we are continually influenced and shaped by the world in which we function. We each have the potential to develop 'a more inclusive, differentiated, permeable, and integrated perspective' (Mezirow, 1991, p. 155). But we also have the possibility of becoming increasingly closed, disillusioned, and fragmented. To develop, that is, to change in the direction of our potential, we must function within an environment that fosters, or at least permits, such development. Organizations, by and large, do not. In recent years we have seen large numbers of employees dropping out of organizations because they recognize that their own development is in jeopardy. This exodus has been particularly true for women, whose sensitivity to development issues may be heightened by their more recent entry into many parts of organizations. But men as well have begun to recognize that they must make developmental choices that, in many cases, remove them from traditional organizations.

We have created organizations that are often detrimental to the human beings that work in them. Our organizations often engender alienation in employees, inhibit human development and encourage dishonesty and distrust between ourselves and others. I am not speaking only of for-profit corporations, but also of universities, where much of my working life has been spent, not-for-profit organizations and government agencies. With few exceptions, the organizations we have created operate in ways that are antithetical to the work environment that we would choose for ourselves or that we understand to result in healthy adult development.

It is unlikely that organizational members will become more integrated while denying meaningful parts of who they are; unlikely that they will become more permeable (open) while daily hiding what they are doing. As adults we spend most of our lives in organizations, certainly most of our waking hours. If we are to continue to develop, it will happen at work; if it cannot happen there, it will probably not happen. It is ironic that the amazing capability of the human mind has created complex organizations that in turn stifle the growth and well-being of those that created them.

The examples of our developmental distress are numerous and familiar. All of us in organizations find ourselves taking actions which we know will not work, while pretending that we are making a good faith effort. We play games with budgets, deliberately padding them, while claiming we need every penny. We deceive others, not out of perversity, but because it is the only way we can find to get our jobs done. We often feel we are being treated like children, particularly when others withhold information or make decisions for 'our own good'; and we, as well, withhold information from others for 'their good'. Such actions have become part of our taken-for-granted assumptions about how we must function in organizations in order to survive and get ahead. We have come to believe that this is 'just the way it is', 'all organizations have politics', 'you just have to play the game.'

Jerry Harvey (1989) created a clever true/false instrument, 'The Phrog Index', that reveals to the respondent some of his or her own debilitating taken-for-granted assumptions. He first elicits a response from us about what we believe about how people in general must function in organizations in order to get the job done. Then he turns the questions back on us to reveal the inconsistency of our response. A few items from the Phrog Index illustrate this point:

- Occasionally, it is necessary for a manager to lie to or deceive others in his/her own organization in order to achieve organizational objectives.   T F
- I work most effectively with those who occasionally lie to me.   T F
- It is important that a manager be objective when dealing with subordinates on matters such as performance appraisal, pay, promotion, and recognition.   T F
- I work most effectively with those who treat me as an object.   T F

If we want organizations to become systems which are able to learn and transform themselves, then these organizations will have to be comprised of sub-systems, individuals, who have been enabled to develop more inclusive, integrated, and differentiated perspectives. Likewise, if we want individuals to develop in these ways, we will have to construct organizations that foster that development. One begets the other.

The lack of focus on the development of the larger system, of which each organization is a sub-system, is as disquieting an issue as is the suppression of individual development. That larger system includes the community, nation and environment.

Bellah *et al.* (1985) note that initially the term corporation implied an organization to whom the government granted special status because it clearly served the public interest. They advocate reasserting the idea 'that incorporation is a concession of public authority to a private group *in return for* service to the public good.' In their opinion such a change would alter 'what is now called the "social responsibility of the corporation" from its present status, where it is often a kind of public relations whipped cream decorating the corporate pudding, to a constitutive structural element in the corporation itself.' (p. 290). They say, 'Management would become a profession in the older sense of the word, involving not merely standards of technical competence but standards of public obligation that could at moments of conflict override obligations to the corporate employer' (p. 290).

This conception of what an organization is or could be is far from the way most organizations currently function in relation to the larger system. Many of our organizations, for example, knowingly sell products that are harmful to other human beings, or act in ways that damage the environment. Many of our organizations buy companies only to break them up and sell off the parts. Many do not pay a fair share of taxes. Many overcharge their governments for products and service.

I am not suggesting that we, as representatives of our organizations, intend harm when we act in such ways, but that our actions are mediated by our taken-for-granted assumptions about organizations that are based for the most part on a mechanical analogy. We view the organization as a kind of machine whose purpose is to serve the ends of the owners or stockholders, while employees are seen as parts of the mechanism that need to be allocated and controlled in order to achieve the owners' ends. If, instead of the mechanical analogy, we were to fully embrace an analogy of the organization as a purposeful social system, we would derive a very different set of actions – a set that fosters learning.

While acknowledging that it is our taken-for-granted assumptions that guide our actions, rather than some sinister intent, we are nevertheless jointly responsible for the organizations we have created. Top management of any organization bears some responsibility, but so does each and every organizational member who colludes through silence or through the acceptance of their own powerlessness. The resolution of these difficulties we have created is also a joint responsibility.

Through collective learning we have the possibility of transforming the organizations we have created, not instantaneously nor without considerable struggle, but in the direction that we choose. Learning is the most potent force for change that exists. It was William James who said, 'The greatest discovery in our generation is that human beings, by changing the inner attitudes of their minds can change the outer aspects of their lives.' Learning, as I will use the term in this book, goes beyond the acquisition of existing knowledge. It is an approach to human functioning that emphasizes the intention to 'make sense of' our world and to act responsibly upon the understanding we derive from that sense-making. Understanding without action is impotence, and action without understanding is foolish.

I am not suggesting that we, as individuals, can change our organizations. I have fallen on my own sword too many times to hold such a belief. It is the learning of the collective that, for me, holds this possibility – what Bohm (1990) calls social intelligence. That intelligence is at the heart of democracy and self-governance. Jefferson said, 'I know of no safe depository of the ultimate powers of the society but the people themselves, and if we think them not enlightened enough to exercise their control with a wholesome discretion, the remedy is not to take it from them, but to inform their discretion.' The truism that a percentage of our workforce does not want the responsibility of self-governance, while it may be accurate, does not relieve them or us of the responsibility to learn, that is to 'make sense of' our world and to act responsibly upon the understanding we derive from that sense-making.

As a global society we have been learning, slowly and falteringly – the Berlin wall fell, the totalitarian government of the Soviet Union gave way. We are learning together that we must act to save the planet, that we must eliminate nuclear weapons, that we must recycle our waste. It is extremely difficult for a global society, with all of its diversity, to learn. It is difficult for nations to learn; yet they can and do learn. South Africa is learning about its own injustice; the USA is learning about how to conserve rather than exploit its environment. Organizations can learn as well. And if we can get better at collective learning at the organizational level we may be able to use that understanding to increase our ability to learn at the national and societal level.

Learning is the most magnificent gift we have as human beings. It is a gift we have customarily thought of as an individual capability. Framing learning in that way, we have used our minds to do great things–create glorious music and art, write wonderful books, develop incredible technology, build intricate theories that explain the whole of the universe, and much more.

When we reframe learning as a collective as well as an individual capability, we amplify its power. With such power we might be able to address some of the social issues that are so pervasive and troublesome. We are not without tangible evidence of the power of collective learning. At the micro level the research on learning demonstrates its potency. At the macro level we have the hopeful worldwide trends toward democracy, conservation, health and unity.

However, to make use of collective learning we need to understand it better. It is my hope that this book will make a contribution to that effort – knowledge about how and why collective learning works. A part of that understanding is the way collective learning is related to individual learning. In much of the literature they are treated as two separate phenomena, related only by analogy. This book tries to explicate that relationship.

Chapter 1 considers why organizational learning has caught our attention at this time. I suggest two major factors that necessitate the emphasis on collective rather than individual learning: the changing nature of work that is a result of the dawning Knowledge Age, and the increasing pace of change which often invalidates known answers and demands that we continually learn. In this chapter I operationally define organizational learning and outline the major implementation constructs that are implied in the definition.

Chapters 2, 3 and 4 address some of the difficult questions that organizational learning raises. Who learns? By what process does the learning occur? Does an organization have a mind with which it learns? Is organizational learning simply a heuristic or is it an accurate description of a social system? I start from the position that organizational learning is an extrapolation of the concept of individual learning. Thus, any model of organizational learning must be based in, and be compatible with, individual learning theory. To build this relationship I articulate a theory of individual learning in Chapter 2 and from that derive a possible model of how organizational learning occurs in Chapter 3.

Chapter 4 describes an organizational learning cycle. Three case examples, Chaparral Steel, The World Health Organization and Johnsonville Foods illustrate the cycle.

Chapter 5 describes the organizational learning cycle in greater depth, adding examples from other organizations. Where available, I provide theory and research data to support the organizational learning cycle.

Chapter 6 discusses the ways organizations are attempting to accelerate the learning cycle. Examples of Weisbord's (1992) strategic search conferences, GE's Work-Out, Wal-Mart's QMI and Open Space Technology are included.

Chapter 7 talks about the need to change the way we develop managers if we want development programs to be compatible with, indeed to support, organizational learning. This chapter may be of particular interest to human resource professionals who are charged with the task of designing learning experiences for managers.

Chapter 8 describes the culture that promotes organizational learning. I have framed this discussion around many of the basic organizational assumptions suggested by Schein (1992).

Chapter 9 draws the relationship between organizational learning and the democratization of organizations. I have talked about why and how organizational learning leads not only to greater participation, but to the more democratic idea of shared authority.

There are two appendices. Appendix A is a compilation of definitions of organizational learning drawn from the literature. I note the major similarities and differences across the definitions. Appendix B is a glossary of terms, most of them introduced in Chapters 2 and 3. I started writing this book with the firm intent to keep technical terms and certainly jargon to a minimum. Having completed it and contemplated the need for a glossary, I discover I have come nowhere near reaching that goal. The difficulty I found, and which the reader may find as well, is that the term 'learning' has so many meanings that to talk with any clarity about different aspects of learning, I have needed to use differing terms otherwise the whole thing becomes a great muddle. It is necessary, for instance, to differentiate the act of learning from the results of learning. The term 'learning' in common usage implies both things. I offer apologies in advance to the reader and hope the glossary will be of some help in wading through the terms.

Finally, I give my thanks to colleagues who reviewed earlier drafts of the book: Mike Pedler, John Burgoyne, George Roth, Alan Mumford, Ed Blankenhagen and Marty Castleberg.

References

Ackoff, R. L. (1981). *Creating the Corporate Future*. New York: John Wiley & Sons.

Bellah, R.N., Madsen, R., Sulivan, W., Swidler, A. and Tipton, S.M. (1985). *Habits of the Heart*. Berkeley: University of California Press.

Bohm, D. (1990). On Dialogue (transcript) Ojai CA: David Bohm Seminars .

Harvey, J. (1989). *Phrog Index*. (unpublished), The George Washington University.

Mezirow, J. (1991). *Transformative Dimensions of Adult Learning*. San Francisco: Jossey-Bass.

Schein, E. H. (1992). *Organizational Culture and Leadership* (2nd edn). San Francisco: Jossey-Bass.

Weisbord, M.R. and 35 International Coauthors (1992). *Discovering Common Ground*, San Francisco: Berrett-Koehler.

1 Introduction

We have entered the Knowledge Age, and the new currency is learning. It is learning, not knowledge itself, which is critical. Knowledge is the result of learning and is ephemeral, constantly needing to be revised and updated. Learning is 'sense making': it is the process that leads to knowledge. Thurber once said, 'In times of change learners shall inherit the earth, while the learned are beautifully equipped for a world that no longer exists'. Organizational learning requires learning rather than being learned.

Unfortunately, the term 'learning', perhaps because of early school experiences, for most of us has come to mean to 'thoroughly grasp what an expert knows'. For example, when we want to 'learn about' quality we study the processes that someone far more knowledgeable than ourselves, such as Deming, Juran or Crosby, has devised. If we want to 'learn' how to lead, we turn to Bennis, DePree or Blanchard to learn how the experts suggest we lead. We may modify the expert's processes to fit our own situation, but when we talk about learning we are essentially talking about finding and comprehending someone else's *answer*. The premises of this conception of learning are that:

1. There is a right answer.
2. The answer is known.
3. If we can identify the 'knower' and comprehend those ideas, we can apply the answer to achieve our goals.

These are not false premises, but they are limited ones, useful with some types of issues, but inappropriate for others. These premises are most useful when the answers are known and when the problems are stable. The caveat is that for most of the problems that organizations face there are no known answers: they are problems that have never before been experienced, and those problems exist within a context of great turbulence, so that even if we had answers that had worked before, it is not clear that they would fit our changed situation.

Organizational learning is based on a very different set of premises:

1. There are many right answers, as in the concept of equifinality; there are many ways to reach the same goal.
2. People who are concerned about and affected by a problem are capable of developing useful knowledge to resolve it.
3. Learning occurs in a context of work and praxis, and results from intentional effort.

The Relationship Between Learning and Change

A formula borrowed from ecology states that in order for an organism to survive, its rate of learning must be equal to or greater than the rate of change in its environment. The formula is written $L \geqslant C$. Considering organizations as organisms, it is apparent that organizations are going to have to increase their rate of learning to survive in these times of unprecedented change.

The formula, however, does not acknowledge our human ability to change the environment as well as adapt to it. It is commonly held that change is caused by forces over which organizations have little control. However, the reality is that we create much of the change to which we must then adapt – for example, we create technological change, alter gender relations and create multinational organizations. We are unique, of all creatures on the face of the earth, in that we can not only respond to, but also alter, our environment (Botkin *et al.*, 1979).

Not only can we physically change our environment, we can alter it by reframing or reconceptualizing it. Weick (1979) uses the term 'enactment' to indicate the reciprocal influence between organizations and their environment. In part, the concept of enactment implies a self-fulfilling prophecy: the perceiver tends to see what is expected. But the concept of enactment goes further, to suggest that the organization implants meaning on the mass of data available and thereby creates the environment in which it will function.

Knowledge that we create through learning allows us to change our environment, whether by reframing it, physically altering it or both. The two factors, learning and change, reinforce each other. The faster the rate of change the more new knowledge we must create to deal with the change; the more knowledge we create the faster we change our world. Friedlander (1983) says, 'Learning is the process that underlies and gives birth to change. Change is the child of learning' (p. 194).

It is certainly possible for change to occur without being preceded by learning. A hurricane, a hostile takeover or new government regulations all can necessitate organizational change. When such change occurs it is followed by organizational learning, even when it was not preceded by it.

Change is preceded by organizational learning when, for example, an organization learns from its customers that product change is needed, it comes to understand that its reward structure is not effective, or it envisions a desired future toward which it chooses to strive. Organizational learning can lead to change which can lead to more organizational learning.

Organizational learning then, can lead to the continuous transformation of an organization and its environment. However, that transformation is not the familiar one-step process of moving from state A, which has been deemed insufficient, to state B, the better way. Organizational learning does not define an end state, but rather is the process that allows the organization to continually generate new states, as in A to B to C to D, and so on. No organizational problem stays solved for long, because each solution engenders a new problem. The key to organizational learning is not only the ability of the organization to transform itself and its environment, but to do so continuously (see Fig. 1.1).

Figure 1.1   Planned versus continuous change.

The Changing Nature of Work

Whether the Knowledge Age began with the popularization of the personal computer, as Zuboff (1988) would have it, or with the creation of the GI Bill (that sent returning soldiers back to universities), as Drucker (1992) assumes, it is certain that it is here. In the 1990s, to work in an organization is more likely to mean manipulating information than raw materials. The vast majority of jobs require individuals to interpret, analyse, and/or synthesize information. Where in the past such requirements were asked only of high-level managers, they are now demanded of workers at all levels. The terms 'interpretation', 'analysis' and 'synthesis' are often used as synonyms for learning; thus learning and work have become synonymous terms. 'As noted by Howell and Cooke (1989), smart machines increase the cognitive complexity of the tasks performed by the human being. Instead of simple procedural and predictable tasks, the human becomes responsible for inferences, diagnoses, judgment, and decision making, often under severe time pressure' (Goldstein and Gilliam, 1990, p. 139). Rather than learn in preparation for work, *employees must learn their way out of the work problems they address.*

The role of the person who supervises such ambiguous work has also changed; managers can no longer rely on control, but must find leverage in jointly establishing direction and goals. Learning creates equals, not subordinates, and thus work is increasingly conceived as a team effort. In past decades it was possible to teach workers how to do a specific task and then set them to doing it. Managers were responsible for making sure the workers were following the procedure they had been taught, a control task. It is, however, not possible for managers to provide such specific instruction for the task of interpreting, synthesizing and analysing information. Rules, to the extent they can be provided at all, are more useful as a heuristic that offers guidance but cannot provide answers. In this sense, knowledge workers more closely resemble the self-employed than they do a conventional workforce (Drucker, 1992).

Perelman (1984) notes: 'By the beginning of the next century, three quarters of the jobs in the U.S. economy will involve creating and processing knowledge. Knowledge workers will find that continual learning is not only a prerequisite of employment but is a major form of work' (p. xvii). Zuboff (1988), in her book *In the Age of the Smart Machine*, explains that information technology has altered basic assumptions about the relationship between work and learning. She says,

> Learning is no longer a separate activity that occurs either before one enters the workplace or in remote classroom settings. Nor is it an activity preserved for a managerial group. The behaviors that define learning and the behaviors that define being productive are one and the same. Learning is not something that requires time out from being engaged in productive activity; learning is the heart of productive activity. To put it simply, learning is the new form of labor. (p. 395)

It is customary to think of learning and work as being separate activities, the former preceding the latter. Zuboff suggests that more often learning is the work task. Zuboff considers 'intellective skills,' which are the ability to make meaning and exercise critical judgement, as the organization's most precious resource. The organization's investment in upgrading and maintaining those skills is comparable with that of investing in technology itself.

It is the recognition of these two factors, the changing nature of work and the increased rate of change itself, that prompts organizations to view learning as a more critical variable than it might have been in the past. Organizations are trying to figure out how to improve their processes, transfer best practices from one part of the organization to another, more quickly incorporate new technologies, make collective use of what their sub-systems know – all learning tasks.

Defining Organizational Learning

For the purposes of this book I shall define organizational learning as 'the intentional use of learning processes at the individual, group and system level to continuously transform the organization in a direction that is increasingly satisfying to its stakeholders'.

The complexity of this definition suggests some need for decoding. The definition begins with the term 'intentional'. All organizations learn to a greater or lesser extent; they adapt to environmental constraints, prevent the repetition of past mistakes and generate innovative, new ideas. Although such organizational learning examples occur, equally typical are situations in which learning is not achieved, that is, organizations repeat their mistakes, fail to adapt to customer needs, and are unable to improve their processes to meet rising competitive standards. Even when organizational learning does occur, it is often accidental rather than as the result of intention. Lacking intentional processes at the individual, group and system levels to facilitate organizational learning, most organizations are inefficient learners and much that could be learned is lost or missed.

In common usage the term 'learning' has two related but very different meanings. It is often used as a noun, as in 'What did you learn from your experience?'. Its meaning in this context could be equated with knowledge, that is, the result of an effort of comprehension. At the collective level, in using the term in the context of knowledge, we might ask 'What has the organization learned from past experiences?'

The second way the term 'learning' is used is as a verb, as in 'to learn'. Here the reference is to processes, as in 'She is a good learner' or 'I am learning a new word processing program'. At the collective level we might use the term 'learning' as a process to ask, 'What do we need to do to be able to correct our mistakes as we go along?' or 'How might we go about understanding this better?' In the definition provided above, and indeed throughout the book, I am using the term in the latter sense rather than the former. Organizational learning, as I am using the term, is the processes the organization employs to gain new understanding or to correct the current understanding; it is not the accumulated knowledge of the organization. This is a non-trivial differentiation from my perspective. A major premise of this book is that learning is the construction and reconstruction of meaning and as such it is a dynamic process. Accumulated knowledge, then, is of less significance than are the processes needed to continuously revise or create knowledge. Those processes can be viewed as a cycle that starts with (1) the widespread generation of information, (2) integrates the new information into the organizational context, (3) collectively interprets the information and (4) then authorizes organizational members to take responsible action based on the interpreted meaning. The fourth step then feeds into the first to generate new information.

The first step includes the process through which the organization acquires information, including whose responsibility it is, and the diversity of the sources of information from which it is gained. This step also involves building learning processes into any organizational action or event so that organizational members learn through it as well as accomplish it. It implies experimentation and self-correction. The second step deals with the speed, accuracy and extent of the dissemination of information; who receives what information and when? The third step comprises the processes that are in place to facilitate organizational members interpreting information. Receiving information and making sense of it are very different processes. Learning has not occurred until organizational members make sense of the information. Because organizational learning involves collective rather than only individual interpretation, that process cannot be left to chance, but requires organized processes. Finally, when organizational members work to make sense of information they need the authorization to act on that understanding. This step implies local rather than centralized control.

Organizational learning requires all four steps of the

organizational learning cycle. It is not sufficient to focus on only one of the two steps, because any one without the others is ineffective. For example, if organizational members collectively interpret a situation but their learning is not informed by accurate information, the learning is ineffective. Likewise, if organizational members learn ways to improve their organizational actions but are unable to put to use their new understandings, the learning itself is wasted.

The purpose of the organizational learning cycle is the *continuous transformation* of the organization. Earlier I differentiated continuous transformation (A to B to C to D) from change as a one time event (A to B). The learning processes that are useful in furthering continuous transformation are considerably different from those needed to create a specific change. For the latter the need is to be able to articulate the desired new state, to identify the gaps between the desired and current states and to define steps to close the gap. For continuous change the focus is on the processes that inform and facilitate ongoing change: on the process rather than the destination, recognizing that the destination is only one stop on a longer journey.

To define the term 'organization' I rely on Argyris and Schon (1978). They begin their book, entitled *Organizational Learning*, by asking, 'What is an organization that it can learn?' They explain that a group of people becomes an organization when the individuals which comprise it develop procedures for:

1. Making decisions in the name of the collective.
2. Delegating to individuals the authority to act for the collective.
3. Setting boundaries between the collective and the rest of the world.

By contrast, they depict a mob as a collective of people which may run about and shout but cannot make a decision or take an action in its own name. Until rules or procedures are in place, each individual can act for him- or herself but cannot act in the name of the collective, cannot say 'We have decided'. For the collective to act, members must have an identified vehicle for collective decision-making and action. When members have created such rules and procedures they can be said to have organized.

A collective comes together to form an organization in order to accomplish a complex task, one which is too complex for any one individual to accomplish. The organization defines a strategy for decomposing that complex task into simpler components which are regularly delegated to individuals (e.g. president, computer programmer, welder). The organization's task system is a pattern of interconnected roles which is both a design for work and a division of labour. The task system operates through a set of norms, strategies and assumptions which specify how the work gets divided and how the tasks get performed. Such norms, strategies and assumptions include what an acceptable margin of profit is, ways in which communication occurs, who gets promoted, what market to target and how resources are allocated. Although these norms, strategies, and assumptions, perhaps even more than the rules for deciding and acting, may be tacit rather than explicit, they nevertheless guide the way the organization accomplishes its tasks (Argyris and Schon, 1978).

The final part of the definition states 'in a direction that is increasingly satisfying to its stakeholders'. The implication here is a political one – referencing who defines the ends for which the organization strives as well as who defines the means to reach those ends. I am arguing that when information is widely shared and when organizational members use 'intellective skills' and are encouraged to challenge the organization's assumptions, they will also question the ends toward which the organization is striving and will insist upon a shared responsibility in their definition. Moreover, I am suggesting that it is not only organizational members but all of the stakeholders of an organization who must be considered in defining those ends.

The argument that I make in this book is that by employing the processes of the organizational learning cycle organizations can transform themselves. Moreover, the act of organizational learning carries with it a kind of emancipation from hierarchically controlled organizations and engenders greater self-governance and responsibility.

References

Argyris, C. and Schon, D. A. (1978). *Organizational Learning: A Theory of Action Perspective*. Reading MA: Addison-Wesley.

Botkin, J., Elmandjra, M. and Malitza, M. (1979). *No Limits to Learning*. Elmsford NY: Pergamon Press.

Drucker, P. F. (1992). The new society of organizations, *Harvard Business Review*, September/October, 95–104.

Friedlander, F. (1984). 'Patterns of Individual and Organizational Learning' in Srivastva, Suresh and Associates, *The Executive Mind, New Insights on Managerial Thought and Action*, pp. 192–220. San Francisco: Jossey-Bass Inc.

Goldstein, I. L. and Gillian, P. C. (1990). 'Training System Issues in the Year 2000'. *American Psychologist*, (45) 2, pp. 134–143.

Perelman, L. (1984). *The Learning Enterprise: Adult Learning, Human Capital and Economic Development*. Washington DC: The Council of State Planning Agencies.

Weick, K. E. (1979). *The Social Psychology of Organizing*. New York: Random House.

Zuboff, S. (1988). *In the Age of the Smart Machine*. New York: Basic Books.

2 A Theoretical Framework of Individual Learning

Understanding how we as individuals make sense of the world is at the core of our understanding of how the collective learns. The processes we design for organizational learning must take into account the immense capability as well as the peculiar limitations of individual learning. For example, later in this chapter I shall describe the sizeable amount of individual learning that is tacit. If, in designing ways that sub-systems of the organization can learn best practices from each other, we ignore the tacit aspects of learning, we shall construct ineffective processes. Likewise, if we misconceive of individual learning as the passive receipt of information, we might not design into the task of teams the necessary procedures that would allow them to self-correct.

In this chapter I go into considerable detail about how individual learning occurs. I outline how we take in data, how we make meaning of it, and the configuration in which cognitive psychologists postulate that it is stored. I talk about some of the surprising foibles of the human mind – those that get us into trouble but which are paradoxically our greatest strength. I discuss the relationship between what we 'know' and what we think of as truth as well as the relationship between what we know and how we act. I look at meta-cognition, our active monitoring of our learning processes, and finally I discuss the relationship between learning and development.

The extensive detail in this chapter is in part because learning is a complex topic that requires substantial explication if it is to be useful to us in understanding collective learning. But I must confess that my own fascination with learning is equally to blame for the length of the chapter. It is, I find, the most human of capabilities. Perry (1970) says that what an organism does is organize; and what a human organism organizes is meaning. I marvel at what we, as the human race, have been able to achieve because we are such good learners, and I marvel at how easily we are blinded by constructions of our own making. William Blake said it most eloquently:

> I wander thro' each charter'd street
> Near where the charter'd Thames does flow,
> And mark in every face I meet
> Marks of weakness, marks of woe.
>
> In every cry of every Man
> In every Infant's cry of fear,
> In every voice, in every ban,
> The mind-forg'd manacles I hear
>
> *London*

The theory that is discussed in this chapter is based on a constructionist's view of cognition, one of several individual learning theories that I could have employed in such an explanation. A constructionist view of learning starts from the position that learning is the act of interpreting experience, that interpretation is unique to each individual and is both enabled and constrained by the individual's process of sense making. In this chapter I have relied heavily on the ideas of Robert Gagné, John Anderson and Gregory Bateson. The ideas of Chris Argyris have been incorporated as well. Although not generally thought of as a learning theorist, Argyris's work is in agreement with cognitive constructionist theories of learning and, moreover, his work has focused on the intersection between individual and organizational learning.

For many of us the term 'learning' is associated with school or with studying for a difficult test. In this chapter I address learning in a much broader sense, because only a small part of what we, as individuals, 'know' is learned in a school setting. As an example, when McCall *et al.* (1988) investigated how executives learned what they knew about managing, the executives attributed less than 5 per cent to classroom instruction. If we are to use the concept of individual learning to help us understand organizational learning, we will have to address learning in its broadest sense: that which occurs through our everyday experience.

**The Difference
That Makes a
Difference**

There are three ways that we as individuals come to know something:

1. Direct experience (the receipt of sensory data such as colour, sound and pain).
2. Verbal transmission of information (ideas voiced by others, reports, books, formulas etc.).
3. The reorganizing of what we already know into a new configuration.

Differentiating between direct experience, verbal transmission and reorganization of existing meaning does not imply that the process of learning associated with each is separated in time or space. In fact, most learning involves all three simultaneously. For example, as we listen to the explanation of a concept that a colleague offers, we also make inferences based on the intensity with which the individual speaks as well as the accompanying facial and hand gestures.

As human beings we take in only a small part of the information that exists in the world around us. Therefore we cannot lay claim to creating an accurate reproduction of the world in our own minds. Our human sensory equipment is, for example, limited both in terms of the range of sound and the range of light waves that it can perceive; humans cannot see X-rays nor hear a whistle pitched for the ears of a dog. Much of what goes on in the world goes unheeded and unnoticed by us as human beings: it is too small or too vast, too high or too low, too fast or too slow.

Even that class of data which our limited sensory equipment is capable of registering is filtered through our selective attention, which causes us to focus on certain data and to ignore others. For example, we ignore background noise in a movie, we fail to notice who is sitting in most of the cars that are passing us on the highway, and we do not notice what others in the restaurant are wearing. That attention involves a selection process does not imply that it is always intentional selection. Selection is, in fact, most often not under our conscious control. Our sensory receptors appear to be constructed so as to automatically attend to changes in level of intensity that would indicate new data are in the environment: for example, a change in volume, or the movement of an object. It is 'differences' that draw our attention and that are registered by our sensory receptors (see Fig. 2.1).

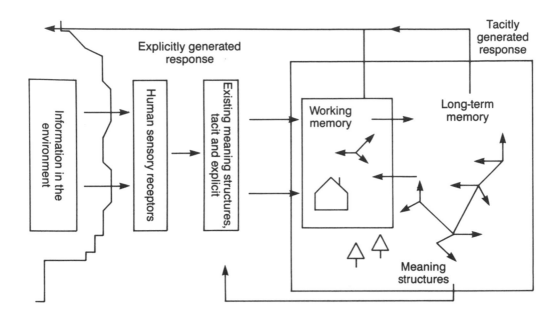

Figure 2.1   Development of meaning structures in individuals.

In a conceptual sense, as well, learning is about differences. We attend to that which is different from our current understanding and from our expectations: for example, we notice a friend's behaviour that has changed or that is outside of the norm of what we consider acceptable behaviour, or we notice an attitude that a new acquaintance holds that differs markedly from our own. We give attention to a goal that we fell short of reaching. Difference may be produced internally, as in two conflicting ideas we hold, or it may occur between ourselves and the environment (in which I include others). The absence as well as the presence of something can represent difference to us – a letter that was not received or food which is unavailable are differences we notice. However, to learn from difference, we must internalize it. A whistle that is at a pitch too high for us to hear does not represent a difference between silence and the whistle. The proverbial frog, who willingly sat in the pot of water that gradually came to a boil, did not internalize the difference in temperature, except in the most literal sense. 'Information' as Gregory Bateson (1979) says, 'consists of differences that make a difference' (p. 105). To learn we must be able to hold the difference within our minds long enough to make sense of it.

Interpreting and Organizing Data

We create 'meaning structures' from the data that we encounter in our interaction in the world. Meaning structures are ways we organize data in order to make sense of it. Developing meaning structures is a function of seeing relationships in data, such as what is larger or smaller, what is similar to something else, what belongs to the same category, what cause produces what effect, and what comes first, second and third in a sequence.

The word 'data' as I have used it here could leave the mistaken impression that a bit of reality (data) exists in the external world which we perceive, take in and then categorize. However, I intend quite a different meaning. We do not record data that are in the environment, but rather we receive sensory impressions of a subset of the data and then interpret those sensory impressions. It is out of this interpretation that we create meaning structures.

A useful analogy is an inkblot. An inkblot is simply a pattern of light and dark which has no inherent meaning (see Fig. 2.2). What I 'see' in the inkblot is an interpretation I give to the light and dark pattern. Others will interpret the light and dark pattern in different ways. There is no 'right' way to interpret the inkblot, no meaning it 'really' contains. Similarly, what each individual 'sees' in the world is an interpretation of the immense mass of data which exists. As with the inkblot, what we 'see' in the world may be influenced by numerous factors, including the current context in which it is 'seen', meaning structures we have created in the past and genetic factors. Each of us, then, constructs the world and for each of us the construction is different. In a sense learning is about giving meaning to the world. Paulo Freire (1970), the great Brazilian educator and revolutionary, referred to learning as 'naming the world', and in a real sense this is what learning is: creating order and giving meaning to the world.

Figure 2.2   An inkblot.

Each of us having a unique interpretation of the world is an obvious inhibitor to communication. When we talk together about some subject such as 'leadership' your understanding may be based on such a different meaning structure from mine that it makes it hard for us to understand what each other means. It is little wonder that we must work so hard at communication. But the uniqueness born of individual interpretation has very positive and important consequences as well. It is because we each construct the world, rather than mentally copy or record it, that we are able to generate diverse new ideas and understandings. This diversity, created by each person's unique construction of the world, makes us, as a species, creative and intelligent. And further, it is this difference between these individual interpretations that stimulates further learning.

We create meaning structures both intentionally and unintentionally. Meaning structures are created intentionally when we are purposively trying to understand or learn something. I will call that 'comprehension activity'. The unintentional creation of meaning structures occurs outside of our conscious awareness: 'tacit comprehension'. Although the latter is more frequent, the former is more fully understood, so we shall address it first.

Comprehension activity takes place in a metaphorical processing space referred to as 'working memory' (sometimes misnamed 'short-term memory'). In this space, relationships are developed between parts of data that we have taken in. Meaning structures that we have developed in the past are retrieved and are related to the new meaning that is being developed. The reconstructed meaning is then stored in a metaphorical space called 'long-term memory'. Long-term memory contains all that we 'know'. But what we know is not stored in the syntax of spoken language; rather, it is stored as an expanding set of relationships, any one bit of data having relationships to many other bits of data in a web-like configuration. Meaning structures built of multiple relationships allow for a kind of flexibility that could not occur with natural language storage. And flexibility is paramount, because we alter our meaning structures each time we retrieve them to relate them to new data.

I use the term 'metaphorical' because researchers do not postulate a literal space where either working or long-term memory reside. The terms to describe this metaphorical space are borrowed from computer language, so we are using the computer, which we understand, to illustrate what happens in the human process of learning, which we understand much less well. By using the computer as an analogy, we facilitate our thinking about learning, but we also constrain it. The computer is a linear, sequential processor, while human learning is both linear and holistic. Our learning is linear, in that much is comprehended through the linear media of spoken and written language, but we are also able to grasp the subtleness of non-verbal meaning and the context in which an event is occurring in a holistic way, which the computer cannot do.

The meaning structures we develop are linked with other meaning structures to form networks. In this way everything we know is somehow related to everything else we know. The whole of one individual's network is his or her 'cognitive map'. When I use the term 'cognitive' here, I am not intending to limit the relationships to areas of formal knowledge, nor to that which is only in conscious awareness, but I include as well all the feelings, beliefs, motor skills, procedures, and a host of unnamed expressions of our understanding. We have no term to represent all of what we know. We are so used to dividing our knowing into knowledge and feelings. But by using the term cognitive map, I intend to encompass both feelings and knowledge, both tacit and explicit.

The more ways a meaning structure is tied (i.e. ways in which it is related) to our existing cognitive map the more likely we are to be able to retrieve it at a later time. It is difficult to retrieve a new meaning structure that bears little relationship to the existing cognitive map: for example, foreign words, scientific terms or directions that include unfamiliar landmarks are difficult to retrieve after a few minutes because we have few ways to connect these to what is already in our long-term memory. But that also means that the more we learn (that is the larger our cognitive map and the more the meaning structures within it are interrelated) the more we increase our capacity to learn – the capability of tying new information to the cognitive map is increased. So rather than filling up our long-term memory over time, we are increasing its storage capability.

Figures 2.3–2.6 show a very simplistic example of the process of creating meaning structures. Figure 2.3 is a representational map of the meaning structures (relationships between data) in a small part of Sharon's total long-term memory. Sharon has developed meaning structures related to the off-the-shelf products which her company sells. In the map each data bit is related in several different ways to other bits of data. Those relationships are shown with arrows

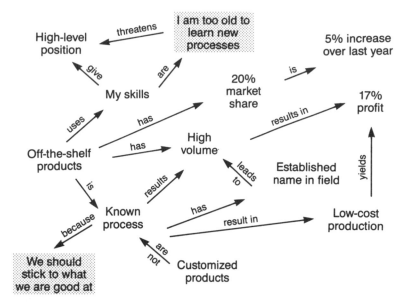

Figure 2.3   Sharon's long-term memory.

and the nature of each relation is indicated by the label on the arrow. We might summarize the interpretation Sharon has given to the data she has about off-the-shelf products as:

> Our company has 20% of the off-the-shelf product market which is a 5% increase over last year. We are able to obtain this high volume, which has resulted in 17% profit, because we have developed a low-cost process. We have an established name in the field that gives us this high volume. We should stick to what we know how to do well. I have the skills needed in the off-the-shelf product business and that has resulted in my obtaining a high-level position in this organization. We should not get into the customized products business, about which we have little understanding.

In Fig. 2.4 we see the same map along with some new information that Jack is providing for Sharon and others at a briefing. By the facts and figures Jack provides he appears to be advocating that the company consider developing a line of customized products given that there is a new technology that could lower production costs for customized products.

In Fig. 2.5 we again see the same segment of Sharon's long-term memory, alongside the information that Jack is providing, and an illustration of how Sharon is relating data in her working memory to the new information. We see that

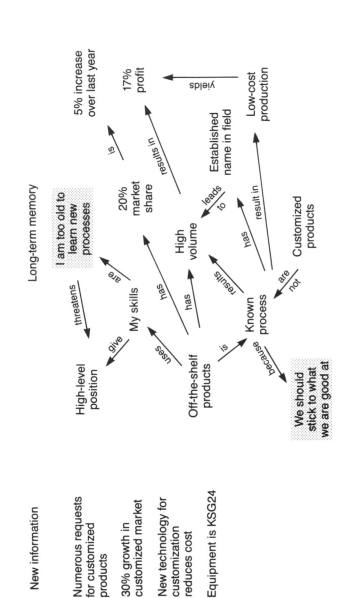

New information

Numerous requests
for customized
products

30% growth in
customized market

New technology for
customization
reduces cost

Equipment is KSG24

Figure 2.4   Introduction of new information into Sharon's current understanding.

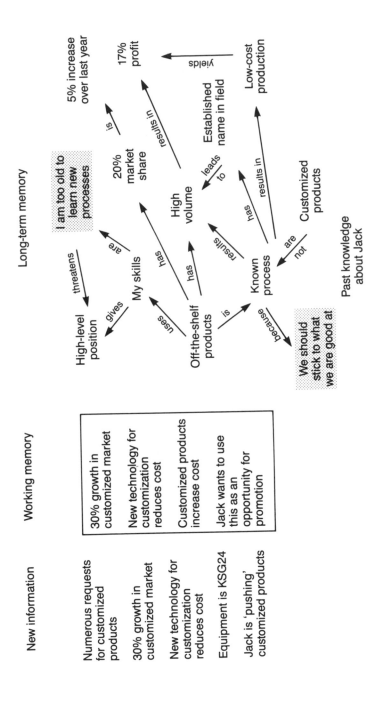

Figure 2.5   Integration of new information into Sharon's long-term memory.

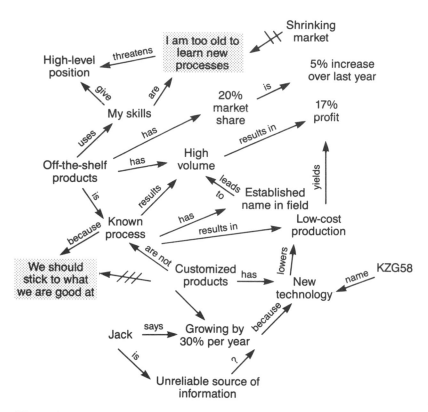

Figure 2.6   Revised map of Sharon's long-term memory.

she has taken in some, but not all, of what Jack said and is retrieving related meaning structures from her own long-term memory that are related to what Jack has said.

The final figure in this series (Fig. 2.6) again shows Sharon's long-term memory, now reconstructed with some of Jack's information. Her reconstructed map includes the idea that this new technology may make customized products lower cost, but includes as well some doubts about the information because of what she knows of Jack from the past. The new information also appears to have raised some confusion for her about whether the company should stick to what it knows how to do (illustrated by the slash marks across the arrow). These figures illustrate Sharon's comprehension activity as she attempts to make sense of new data she has taken in and to relate it to the meaning structures which she already has in long-term memory.

We may construct meaning structures intentionally, as described in this example. However, we have another way of learning that is less volitional, although it still involves the development of relationships and their storage in long-term memory. This second way of learning occurs over time and without conscious awareness. It is the way young children, for example, learn language, by hearing it and creating patterns in the words and syntax, yet remaining unaware of the patterns. The child is aware only that he or she is able to communicate, but not of the syntax learned to facilitate the construction of sentences.

It is not only children who learn tacitly. Much of the knowledge we as adults carry about ourselves and others is learned through tacit comprehension. Our ideas about abstractions such as beauty, justice, love and freedom have been learned tacitly from exposure to the culture in which we live. When we join a new organization as an adult employee, we learn how to act, what to say and what is expected. Much of this cultural information is learned, not by someone conveying it verbally, but from working in the organization over a period of time. A young woman, just out of law school who has recently joined a firm, may find herself 'acting like a lawyer' without ever having made a conscious decision to act differently than she did as a student. She has learned these new behaviours through tacit comprehension.

Our meaning structures take many forms including visual and auditory images, rules, concepts, beliefs about people and ourselves, attitudes and values, motor skills, inferences, and rules for thinking. Meaning structures are also constructed about feelings, such as hate, love, joy, awe and anger; beauty, as in music, art and dance; and images, such as faces, gestures and shapes. The smell of vanilla may be related to an idea, the emotion experienced upon hearing Beethoven's *Ode to Joy* may be related to a person or an event and the sight of the Lincoln Memorial may be related to our sense of freedom or justice. All that we know we know, and all that we do not know we know, but do know, is stored as meaning structures.

I have used the word 'stored', but the image of putting an object into storage, which is later retrieved looking much the same as when we put it in, would be an inaccurate picture of how we store and retrieve meaning. Meaning that is retrieved from long-term memory is always reconstructed. We alter the relationships between parts in the retrieval process. An analogy might be rather than retrieving your bicycle from the closet, you select from a whole closet full of parts and build up the bicycle each time you retrieve it. The general shape of the bicycle might be consistent, but the particular wing nuts, seat or frame colour might differ each time. Thus, we construct our remembrances. No wonder they vary so greatly in the telling.

Learning and truth

The representational map of Sharon's long-term memory (Fig. 2.6) shows that the name she has related to the new technology is KZG58. The name Jack reported at the briefing was KSG24. We can say that this particular relationship stored in Sharon's long-term memory is wrong. And although it is a small inaccuracy, one which she can correct the next time she is exposed to information related to the equipment, it nevertheless illustrates that the meaning structures we build may not be accurate. At another level we could say that perhaps KZG58 would be a more fitting name for the equipment, or even that Sharon knows something about the equipment of which Jack is ignorant. But if, for the moment, we take at face value that Sharon has mis-remembered the name of the equipment, we can say that the meaning structure she has built is inaccurate.

Individuals have a number of human limitations that result in them developing and holding meaning structures which may not be accurate. These include a tendency to look for evidence that supports their initial view rather than seeking disconfirming evidence, to generalize from small samples or single instances (Feld, 1986), and to give greater weight to more recent events. Humans are inclined to perceive the world through the lens of past events, to create self-fulfilling prophecies, and to fail to check out the inferences they make from incomplete data (March *et al.*, 1991).

Even taking into consideration these troublesome human fallacies, the ability that humans have to create relationships and patterns is extraordinary. There are virtually no limits to our understanding – there are always new relationships to build, new ways to 'see' the world. We can, in fact, invent the world with this wonderful ability. We can, as Robert Kennedy did, 'see things that never were'. If our minds were *only* able to record the external world accurately, we would not be able to create such splendid new worlds. If the price of imagination is the human propensity for error, perhaps it is cheap at the cost!

We are, however, still left with the difficult problem of how we can know if the meaning structures we develop are true. Bateson (1979) cautions:

> Let us say that truth would mean a precise correspondence between our description and what we describe or between our

total network of abstractions and deductions and some total understanding of the outside world. Truth in this sense is not obtainable. And even if we ignore the barriers of coding, the circumstance that our description will be in words or figures or pictures but that what we describe is going to be in flesh and blood and action – even disregarding that hurdle of translation, we shall never be able to claim final knowledge of anything whatsoever. (p. 27)

He concludes that we cannot know if our meaning structures are true. Yet, in order to function in the world we must act 'as if' the meaning structures that we have constructed are true. And at the same time we must strive to remember that there are other relationships that we do not see – so that we are ever open to another way of seeing the world. It is all too easy to forget that we have created the world in which we live.

Development of Meaning Structures

The new meaning the individual constructs may confirm or alter the existing meaning structures that the individual has in long-term memory. Much of the data we take in confirms the meaning that we have already constructed. In part this happens because existing meaning structures influence both what the individual attends to or ignores and how data are interpreted. Individuals appear to have a preference for interpreting the world in terms of their existing meaning structures, which is another way of saying we often see what we expect to see. If the individual has developed a meaning structure about Mary, a co-worker, that 'Mary is shy', the individual may interpret many of Mary's actions, both verbal and non-verbal, as examples of her shyness. Another co-worker who has developed a different meaning structure about Mary, for example, 'Mary is aloof' might interpret those same actions as examples of aloofness. Moreover, individuals appear to attend more to information that supports their existing meaning structure than to information that might refute it.

When we notice information that conflicts with our existing meaning structure, we experience an internal sense of discomfort or dissonance. Human beings appear to be strongly motivated to reduce the dissonance created by information that conflicts with existing meaning structures. For example, one of the effective and intentional uses of dissonance in management development programmes is to provide participants with feedback about how others view them, which, if discrepant with how the individuals see their own behaviour, motivates them to change. To reduce the dissonance we experience we can either deny the validity of the new information ('What do they know anyway?') or process the new information comparing it with the existing meaning structures until a new understanding is reached, that is, reconstruct the meaning structures. 'Dissonance' is another way of saying 'difference'. So we are back to the importance of difference to learning.

The Relationship of Meaning Structures to Action

Our actions are mediated by our meaning structures. Action, as the term is used here, includes words as well as a physical response, and even includes instructions to others to carry out some course of action. It is possible for us to construct or reconstruct meaning structures without them resulting in noticeable action. The opposite, however, is not possible; in order for us to take any new action our meaning structures must change in some way. Figure 2.7 illustrates a meaning structure that a member of an organization, Jane, has developed out of her experience in that organization over time: 'The organization rewards individual performance, not teamwork'. We can say that this is what Jane believes or knows or has come to understand. The arrows to the right of this statement illustrate how this meaning structure might mediate certain actions. The first action suggests that holding this meaning might result in Jane refraining from sharing resources with her team members, the second that she might skip some team meetings if they interfere with her own

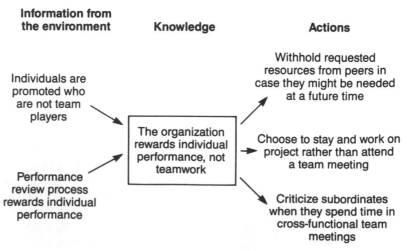

Figure 2.7   The relationship between knowledge and action.

individual performance, and the third that she might put pressure on her subordinates not to spend too much time in cross-functional team meetings. The left-hand column suggests some of the experiences that Jane has had that has led her to construct the meaning structure. She has interpreted these experiences to derive the meaning 'The organization rewards individual performance not teamwork'.

If the organization hopes to change Jane's actions, displayed on the right, Jane will first have to change the meaning structure that is driving her actions. We would not expect, nor want, her to act in ways that did not make sense to her. To change her meaning structure Jane will have to have some new experiences (reflected on the left) that she can interpret in a different way, or perhaps she can reframe that experience as 'past' and, based on the promise of the organization, define the present as different. In any case, it is the meaning she makes that will mediate her actions.

It is of course possible that Jane has other meaning structures, also learned in the context of the organization, that imply that it would be wise to give lip service to teamwork even if she believes the organization does not truly value it. It is such conflicting meaning structures derived from both the mixed messages of the organization and from the undiscussability of such messages that make organizational change so difficult.

Meaning structures, then, mediate action. It is, however, not possible to determine an individual's meaning structures from their actions. Any one action may be mediated by a host of different meaning structures. Jane may attend the team meetings because she values the team, thinks it is expected of her, is trying to get better acquainted with a co-worker, or a host of other reasons. We cannot know what meaning structures an individual has from observing their behaviour.

The Limitations of Working Memory

As human beings we have a limited amount of processing space, and that consideration influences much about the way we learn. Our processing space in working memory appears to be limited to seven (plus or minus two) unrelated bits of data (Miller, 1956). Much more than seven bits and we begin to lose some of the data we are trying to hold on to. Seven digit telephone numbers are about at our limit. It helps to conserve space in working memory if we can put several bits together as one 'chunk', for example, the first three digits of a telephone number chunk as a recognizable section of the community, or five different ways to analyse data we can chunk as 'statistical tools'. When items are chunked we no longer have to hold the individual items but can hold the 'chunk' in our processing space. When we need to we can disaggregate the chunk back into its parts.

The importance of 'chunking', which is another way of saying 'categorizing' data, is that we can then relate larger chunks of data to each other. We are able to build new relationships only among the data which we are able to hold in working memory simultaneously – within our limited processing space. So, the better our ability to chunk data (organize it into categories) the greater the level of complexity with which we can think. Complexity is another way of saying that the individual can find relationships among larger chunks.

Often we find that the more familiar we are with a 'field' of study, the easier it is for us to find categories within it and to find ways those larger categories relate to each other. An example comes from research with chess experts. Surprisingly there is no strategy difference between chess masters and less expert players. Gagné and Glaser (1987) provide this comparison of expert and novice chess players:

> All looked ahead about the same number of moves as they tried to evaluate each move, and used the same strategy to guide this search. However, experts simply recognized the best move and gave it first consideration, evaluating the other moves only as a way of double-checking themselves. When experts look at an apparently complicated situation, they are able to represent it in terms of a small number of patterns or chunks. This ability to perceive the problem in a way that restricts the problem space has since been shown to occur in other areas as well (p. 69).

A second way in which limited processing space influences our learning is that it necessitates making many of our meaning structures *tacit* so that we do not have to deal with them in our conscious awareness. Those meaning structures that we use repeatedly are candidates for becoming tacit, particularly those that do not change much over time. Familiar examples would include motor skills, such as the commands of a word processor or how to work the tricky lock on our door; frequently used interpersonal skills, such as how to respond to a greeting, or react to someone's anger; self-perception, such as how we think about ourselves as smart or kind; and beliefs we hold, such as justice, what is worth striving for, and what is right. To hold such meaning structures tacitly does not mean they are forgotten; rather, they are temporarily lost to conscious awareness.

Actions that are based on tacit meaning structures are *automatic*. They do not need to be thought about, that is they do not need to pass through working memory to be reconstructed and then used. Bateson (1979) says that:

> No organism can afford to be conscious of matters with which it could deal at an unconscious level. Broadly we can afford to sink those sorts of knowledge which continue to be true regardless of changes in the environment, but we maintain in an accessible place all those controls of behaviour which must be modified for every instance. The lion can sink into his unconscious the propositions that zebras are his natural prey, but in dealing with any particular zebra he must be able to modify the movements of his attack to fit with the particular terrain and the particular evasive tactics of the particular zebra (pp. 142–3).

We are often unaware that we have a particular tacit meaning structure until that meaning is challenged. An example of a tacit meaning structure that many organizational members in the USA have held is the appropriateness of upper level management being paid salaries that are up to 100 times greater than first line employees in the same organization. Recently this assumption has been challenged in the media, and thus has come into the conscious awareness of many organizational employees, who have begun to question whether such a differential is appropriate.

A great deal of the interaction that human beings have with each other is informed by tacit meaning structures. Interaction is simply too swift for individuals to take the time to process every aspect of it. Thus, how an individual responds to praise, to disappointment, to confusion, to embarrassment, etc. involves tacit meaning structures. For example, when I want to tell another person that he or she is acting inappropriately, I might make a joke of my criticism. Embedding the criticism in a joke is not a plan that I think through on the spot (as in, 'This person will react less defensively if I make a joke of this than if I am serious'); rather, it is a meaning structure I have developed for dealing with uncomfortable situations and have used frequently enough that it has become tacit and can therefore happen automatically. My exact choice of words may be processed on the spot, but the process of how to tell another person about their inappropriate behaviour may be tacit. Some theorists have suggested that as much as 90% of human meaning structures are tacit.

The benefits of making meaning structures tacit are the freeing up of processing space and the ability to respond more quickly than conscious processing allows. There are, however, serious limitations that tacit meaning structures impose upon our learning as well. One limitation is the difficulty in testing the validity of tacit meaning structures. A second limitation, not unrelated to the first, is the difficulty of changing tacit meaning structures. A third limitation is the propensity to construct and employ untested inferences.

Explicit meaning structures, those that remain in conscious awareness, are put to a kind of test each time we engage in comprehension activity related to them. If a meaning structure we retrieve from long-term memory does not fit new data, and the new data are convincing, we will most likely change the meaning structure before returning it to long-term memory. Functioning in the world provides us with an ongoing check of the explicit meaning we have created for ourselves.

Tacit meaning structures do not, however, receive that continual correction process. We employ tacit structures without recalling them to working memory and without the active comparison to new data. The result is that it is possible to continue employing tacit meaning structures that perhaps worked well for us in the past, but due to changing circumstances no longer do. For example, before the emphasis on quality it was a commonly held axiom that improving quality increased costs. Before the 1980s most organizational members would not have thought about testing that meaning structure.

It is even possible to hold tacit meaning structures that contradict explicit meaning structures. For example, a manager may hold the *tacit* belief that workers need clear and precise directions and the *explicit* belief that workers act more productively if involved in selecting their own goals – and be unaware of the contradiction in the two beliefs. When conflicting meaning structures exist an individual is likely to act in ways that others see as inconsistent. In the above example, employees may interpret the manager's inconsistency as an intent to deceive, when, in fact, the manager may be unaware of the contradiction because of the tacit nature of one of the meaning structures.

Argyris and Schon (1978) go further, to say that not only might we be unaware of the inconsistency between our explicit and tacit meaning structures (they would use the terms 'espoused theories ' and 'theories in use') but that we actually design processes to keep us blind to the discrepancies – and that these designed processes are also tacit. To return to an earlier example in which I used a joke to give negative information to someone. I postulated that the meaning structure which provides the 'joke strategy' is tacit, although the specific language that corresponds with the situation is not. The recipient of the 'joke' is required by norms of politeness to laugh – an implied acknowledgement of the truth of the negative inference of the joke. If the recipient were to take the 'joke' seriously by trying to correct the misperception he or she would be considered a poor sport: after all 'it was only a joke'. The recipient is placed in a position in which the inaccuracy cannot be corrected without the individual appearing to be a poor sport. I, as the joke teller, have effectively designed a process in which it is unlikely that I will receive information that corrects the negative perception I have. And even this process, the process that keeps me blind to my own error, is tacit.

In order to alter tacit meaning structures, it is first necessary to become aware of them – a major problem, since it is difficult to become aware of that of which you are unaware. Perspective appears necessary if individuals are to become aware of that which is tacit. Our tacit meaning structures are like a frame in which we are embedded, and perspective allows us to view ourselves and our actions from outside the frame. Others, who are significantly different from us, can often provide that perspective for us. Working in another country, visiting an organization that is using a process we thought impossible, or sometimes even outdoor adventure programmes, are other ways to gain perspective on our current frame.

To alter a tacit meaning structure we must first become aware of it, and must then be able to recognize the dissonance between it and the new information. We must actively alter the meaning structure and, if it is related to actions that happen rapidly, must practice to make the actions automatic again. It may, in fact, take a lengthy period of time before responses become automatic enough to be useful again in most situations. Anyone who has attempted to use the commands of a new word processing programme, or to employ new communication skills, recognizes in themselves a lack of spontaneity. Until new meaning structures are automatic, interaction responses may, in fact, appear to others to be 'false' or 'put on'.

Finally, the ability humans have to draw inferences from

sparse data is both a great advantage and a considerable problem. To infer means to draw a conclusion. We make hundreds of necessary inferences each day. We predict how people will act from past behaviour; we infer that a problem exists in the accounting department because the statements are late; we infer that there is discrimination because we did not get promoted. Without the ability to draw inferences we would be limited to trial and error learning, never able to make the leaps in thought that can save us time and energy and allow us to deal with significant complexity. The difficulty with inferences comes not because we make them, but because we are inclined to regard our inferences as fact rather than hypothesis. Holding them as fact, we see no need to test them.

Inferences are retained as meaning structures in long-term memory while the original data on which the inference was based are often forgotten. The meaning structure influences the individual's interpretation of future actions and events, thus creating self-fulfilling prophecies. For example, individuals who infer discrimination because they were passed over for promotion are likely to interpret future slights as discrimination and as a result may begin to act in a hostile manner toward those whom they believe are being discriminatory. If the original inference was incorrect, such individuals have now developed a situation in which they are unlikely to discover that. It is also possible that the original inference was correct and discrimination is occurring; because it is an inference does not mean it is incorrect, only that it is untested.

The solution that Argyris and Schon (1978) propose is not to refrain from making inferences, but rather to test our inferences immediately. We typically fail to do that for four reasons:

1. We consider our inferences as fact and therefore see no need to test them.
2. We are embarrassed to talk about the inference, particularly if we hold a negative inference that should turn out to be wrong.
3. We presume that others would be less than truthful about acknowledging the accuracy of our inference or at least be very defensive if it is correct.
4. We cannot see a non-threatening way to test the inference.

Meta-cognition

A type of meaning structure that is of particular importance to the improvement of learning is meta-cognition: our knowledge of our own cognitive processes. Meta-cognition refers to the active monitoring of learning processes, such as self-questioning (Do I now understand this or do I need to read it again?); persistence (how long we will keep trying to make sense of confusing data); relating data sets (asking myself how a piece of equipment (or theory) differs from or is the same as another); purposefully seeking new information (What do I need to learn in order to understand this situation?); and questioning inferences (What data am I basing this inference on and is it adequate?). Meta-cognition functions like an executive controller for our learning. Meta-cognition constitutes our learning style as well as our learning capability. Studies have shown that one thing that differentiates good and poor learners in a school setting is their meta-cognitive skills. Like other parts of our cognitive map, meta-cognition is most often tacit and therefore unavailable for testing.

The Human Need to Learn

As human beings we appear to have a drive to learn that is, in part, a survival mechanism: we function more effectively in a world of which we have made sense (Hatano and Inagaki, 1987). We also derive pleasure from learning; there is a feeling of dissonance associated with confusion (non-understanding) which is relieved in a pleasurable way when we make meaning of ambiguous information.

Learning, however, appears to be about more than survival: it is also about human *development*, the growth of the individual. Maslow (1954) proposes that humans have a drive toward self-actualization, Rogers (1961) talks about basic actualizing tendency, and Kegan (1982) describes the evolving self. Each of these theorists, and many others, characterize development as a progression of 'frames' or lenses through which we interpret our experience. We 'learn' within the context of that frame, altering meaning structures as new information conflicts with current meaning structures. But learning also pushes against the frame, because some of what we experience cannot be understood within the existing frame and remains a nagging dissonance that is difficult to dismiss and impossible to incorporate. At some juncture the frame breaks down – there are too many discrepancies, too much the current frame cannot take into account. A major reorganization of meaning occurs which moves us from one developmental state to the next.

Each stage or period of stability is a way of seeing ourselves in relation to the external world or in the terms we have been using here, a way to organize our understanding of the world and our relationship to it. But as Kegan (1982) has pointed out it is a tenuous and temporary organization structure that we build: 'The relationship gets better organized by increasing differentiations of the self from the environment and thus by increasing integrations of the environment' (p. 113).

Kegan (1982) sees the central theme of this relationship as two basic, but conflicting yearnings of humans, one for communion (the yearning to be included, to be part of, to be close to) and one for agency (the yearning to be autonomous, to be distinct, to choose one's own direction). At various stages we find a satisfactory balance to these two yearnings, favouring one or the other. But over time the balance no longer seems satisfactory and we suffer a period of confusion out of which a new balance is constructed. This conflict between communion and agency is a central construct in many developmental theories, including those of Piaget, Kohlberg, Loevinger, Maslow, Erikson and McClelland.

Learning is central both to bringing about the massive reorganization that causes us to have a new sense of self in relation to the world, and to constructing a satisfactory existence within our current frame.

This need to learn serves many important ends for us as human beings, including survival, both as individuals and as a species, career advancement, prestige, etc. But this need is also simply fundamental to who we are as human beings – we are a learning species. And although there are a considerable number of individuals who suffered so many negative experiences in formal school settings that they no longer think of themselves as learners, they are learners nonetheless.

Summary

There is a long history of theorists who have explored the relationship between experience and learning. John Dewey, Kurt Lewin and Jean Piaget are certainly seminal thinkers and have influenced the ideas of most theorists that have come after them. They inspired the work of later theorists Gregory Bateson, Reg Revans, Paulo Freire, Chris Argyris, David Kolb, Malcolm Knowles, Jack Mezirow and Alan Mumford. I have found Kolb's (1984) model of experiential learning a useful way to summarize the ideas of these theorists and thus helpful in summarizing the process of individual learning outlined in this chapter.

Kolb proposes a cycle through which individual learning progresses (see Fig. 2.8). The cycle begins when we each experience the world through our senses. Kolb calls this step

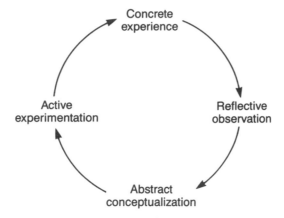

Figure 2.8   Kolb's experiential learning cycle.

'concrete experience', to indicate that he does not mean the vicarious experience we have through books or plays, but a real world experience. Examples of concrete experience could be as varied as sitting through a boring meeting or suffering the distress of losing a job. Kolb suggests that to learn from our experience we must engage in a second step of consciously reflecting on what has occurred. This step he calls 'reflective observation.' We are able to reflect on much less than what occurred in the actual experience. Reflection is selective, and as we saw earlier, is influenced by our expectations and our existing meaning. The third step in the learning cycle is making sense of what we have experienced. In the language of this book that involves relating the new information to existing meaning structures and out of that relationship creating new meaning. Kolb calls this step 'abstract conceptualization'. The final step in Kolb's model is active experimentation. At this step we test out the meaning that we have constructed by taking action in the world – which then leads to new experience. Kolb has shown that over time we tend to get more proficient at some steps of this process than at others, and thus we develop a learning style preference. But, as he has noted, all the steps are necessary, and to the extent that we slight any of the steps, our learning is less effective and complete.

Kolb defines individual learning as 'the process whereby knowledge is created through the transformation of experience'. Although the experiential learning cycle leaves out much of the detail of the learning process that I have described in this chapter, both his definition and the experiential learning cycle capture the essence, which is that:

- Learning is about interpreting what we experience in the world.
- We each create our own unique interpretation.
- The meaning we create mediates our actions.

Individual Learning in the Social Context   In this section I have confined my discussion to how individuals learn, with the intent of using that framework to better understand how a collective might learn. But even in this discussion I have not been able to talk about individuals as isolated entities devoid of contact with others. As the sociologist George Herbert Mead (1934) said, 'Mind can never find expression, and can never come into existence at all, except in terms of a social environment' (p. 223). Individual learning is dependent upon the collective. As we turn now to collective learning we shall see that the converse is also true: collective learning is dependent upon the individual.

References

Argyris, C. and Schon, D. A. (1978). *Organizational Learning: A Theory of Action Perspective*. Reading MA: Addison-Wesley.

Bateson, G. (1979). *Mind and Nature a Necessary Unity*. New York: Ballantine.

Feld, J. (1986). On the difficulty of learning from experience, in Sims, H. P. *et al.* (eds.), *The Thinking Organization*, pp. 263–92. San Francisco: Jossey-Bass.

Freire, P. (1970). *Pedagogy of the Oppressed*. Harmondsworth: Penguin.

Gagné, R. M. and Glaser, R. (1987). Foundations in learning research, in Gagné, R. M. (ed.), *Instructional Technology: Foundations*, pp. 49–83. Hillsdale NJ: Lawrence Erlbaum Associates.

Hatano, G. and Inagaki, K. (1987). A theory of motivation for comprehension and its application to mathematics instruction, in Romberg, T. A. and Stewart, D. M. (eds.), *The Monitoring of School Mathematics*, Background papers, Vol. 2: Implications from psychology; outcomes of instruction. Program Report 87–2, pp. 27–46. Madison WI: Center for Education Research.

Kegan, R. (1982). *The Evolving Self*. Cambridge MA: Harvard University Press.

Kolb, D. A. (1984). *Experiential Learning*. Englewood Cliffs NJ: Prentice-Hall.

March, J. G., Sproull, L. S. and Tamuz, M. (1991). Learning from samples of one or fewer. *Organization Science*, **2** (1), 1–13.

Maslow, A. H. (1954). *Motivation and Personality*. New York: Harper & Row.

McCall, M. W., Lombardo, M. M. and Morrison, A. M. (1988). *The Lessons of Experience*. Lexington MA: Lexington Books.

Mead, G. H. (1934). *Mind, Self, and Society.* Chicago: University of Chicago Press.

Miller, G. A. (1956). The magical number seven, plus or minus two; Some limits on our capacity for processing information. *Psychological Review, 63, 81–97.*

Perry, W. G., Jr. (1970). *Forms of Intellectual and Ethical Development in the College Years.* New York: Holt, Rinehart & Winston.

Rogers, C. R. (1961). *On Becoming a Person: A Therapist's View of Psychotherapy.* Boston: Houghton Mifflin.

A Theoretical Framework for Organizational Learning

Organizations are collections of individuals, each of whom has developed and stored meaning structures, is capable of creating new meaning from their interface with their environment and each other, can test that meaning against their current meaning structures, and can alter or reconstruct their meaning structures – in other words, each organizational member can learn. An organization learns through this capability of its members. Organizational learning is not simply the sum of all that its organizational members know – rather it is the collective use of this capability of learning. It is a verb, not a noun. Argyris and Schon (1978) explain: '. . . there is no organizational learning without individual learning, and that individual learning is a necessary but insufficient condition for organizational learning' (p. 20).

To understand how organizational learning differs from individual learning it is helpful to think of organizational members as having meaning structures that could be categorized as private, accessible and collective (McClellan, 1983) (see Fig. 3.1).

Private, Accessible and Collective Meaning Structures

Not all of any organizational member's cognitive map is available to others in the organization. Those parts of organizational members' cognitive maps which they choose to withhold from other members I shall refer to as 'private meaning structures'. Reasons for retaining as private some of what organizational members know might include a wish to respect information that has been given in confidence, a recognition that certain information could place the individual in a stronger position politically, concern that they might be punished if their mistakes or incompetence were made public, fear of embarrassment if the negative motives they ascribe to others were known, and the assumption that

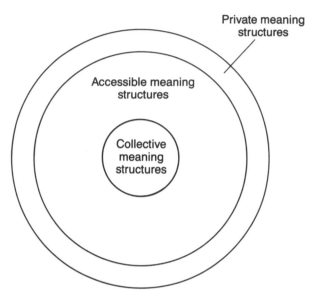

Figure 3.1   Three types of meaning structure.

others are uninterested in their thinking on an issue. Private meaning structures are both explicit and tacit.

Accessible Meaning Structures

Those parts of the individual's cognitive map which he or she is willing to make available to others in the organization I shall call 'accessible meaning structures'. It is through these accessible meaning structures that the organization is able to learn. However, the fact that an individual is willing to make meaning structures accessible does not insure that everyone in the organization will chose to, or be able to, access them. There are time, space, political, intellectual and cultural factors that limit access to others' meaning structures.

The boundaries between accessible meaning structures and private meaning structures are gradual and flexible. For example, individuals may be willing to make their meaning accessible under some circumstances but not under others, or they may be willing to communicate their meaning only to select members of the organization. Thus the same meaning structures may sometimes be private and sometimes accessible.

Figure 3.2 may be a more accurate representation of accessible meaning structures in some organizations than is Fig. 3.1. In large organizations members make certain meaning structures accessible to others within their unit or

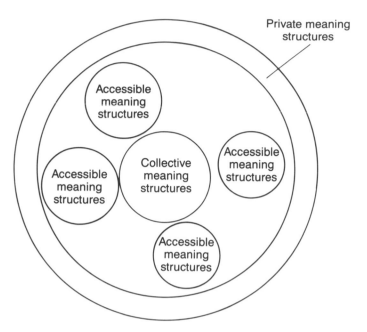

Figure 3.2   Meaning structures in organizations with strong divisional cultures.

division, but may have few, if any, channels to make meaning accessible across unit boundaries.

I have used the term 'accessible meaning structures' here rather than using the more common term of knowledge or information because I want to represent something more encompassing than the conclusions that organizational members have reached. I also want to include within the framework of accessible meaning structures the relationship of those conclusions to other conclusions within individuals' cognitive maps, the logic by which those conclusions were reached, the data that support them, the inferences that were made from them, and the tacit assumptions behind them. Accessible meaning structures are considerably different from what we would normally refer to as information. Information is data that are in-formation, that is the data have been organized into charts, graphs, speech, written statements etc. Information thus organized can reside in many places in the organization, including books, reports, memos and journals, but meaning structures can reside only in human beings. They reside in individuals not as fixed structures but as constantly changing relationships. As we saw in Chapter 2, two different people can examine the same information and construct from it considerably different meaning structures. Although a wide distribution of information is certainly essential for organizational learning, nothing has been learned until organizational members construct their own meaning from the information. Learning, whether organizational or individual, is about the construction of meaning.

Collective Meaning Structures

'Collective meaning structures' are those which organizational members hold jointly with other members of the organization. Collective meaning structures include, but are not limited to, the set of norms, strategies and assumptions which specify how work gets divided and how tasks get performed. Collective meaning structures may be codified in policies and procedures, but to be collective they must also reside in the minds of organizational members.

By using the term 'collective' I do not mean to imply that these meaning structures are precisely the same in each individual. Even when organizational members use the same words to express a norm or belief, such as 'respect for the individual' or 'quality' they often have somewhat different interpretations of those words. By collective, then, I mean there is 'close enough' accord that members function as if there were total agreement. When, however, these collective meaning structures are examined closely, they often reveal significant differences.

Many, although certainly not all, collective meaning structures are tacit. Equivalent to tacit meaning structures at the individual level, tacit collective meaning structures greatly affect how the organization functions. For example, it may be tacitly understood in the organization that whatever else happens you do not miss your schedule, that top management will be selected from individuals with financial backgrounds, that people cover for each other so that everyone can take care of family responsibilities, or that speed is the critical element.

Such tacit collective meaning structures allow the organization to act automatically, swiftly and in concert. There is no need for lengthy discussions, for example, about why we do not miss the schedule – we all simply know to get on with it. Thus, tacit collective meaning structures are very useful to the organization and are in fact necessary. They save time that can be more productively spent on critical issues. Organizations, in fact, attempt through socialization processes and through training to foster collective meaning structures in their members.

Collective meaning structures can, however, also have a negative impact on the organization. In a rapidly changing world meaning structures that were advantageous at one point in time may have become obsolete. If they are tacit, however, there is little discussion about them – they are unavailable for questioning or testing. For example, for many years it was part of General Motors' collective meaning structures that car buyers primarily regarded cars as status symbols. Even when the American public began to buy lower profile Japanese cars, General Motors did not change this collective meaning. It had become tacit and therefore unavailable for testing.

Collective meaning structures make the introduction of new ideas that conflict with the existing collective meaning structures very difficult to implement. A collective meaning structure is often seen, by those who hold it, as 'truth'. It is not questioned because members have no need to question what they know from long years of experience to be true. For example, organizational members may hold a collective meaning structure that union and management of the company are never going to be able to work together cooperatively. This meaning structure influences the way events are interpreted, the willingness to make efforts toward cooperation, the level of trust, etc.

Although the collective meaning structures of an organization do change gradually and continually over time it is difficult to change them radically or suddenly because organizational members continually reaffirm their collective meaning structures to each other. By definition, the collective meaning structures are those meaning structures which all members hold in common. Therefore, interaction between organizational members related to collective meaning structures will lack differences in perspective. When everyone is in agreement there is no one to challenge the accepted position or rationale.

Substantive changes to the collective meaning structures often wait on the appearance of an external force that is novel or discrepant in order to produce adequate dissonance to challenge the agreement. Novel situations might be mergers or technology change. Discrepancies might include organizational decline or criminal incidents. Deliberate requests for fresh thinking might include Strategic Search Conferences (Weisbord *et al.*, 1992), or organizational assessments (Louis and Sutton, 1991).

The process through which the collective meaning structures in the organization change is:

1. Collective meaning structures exist which are not available for dialogue because they have become tacit to organization members.
2. A situation occurs that is novel, or discrepant (the situation may occur spontaneously as a sudden drop in sales or may be induced deliberately as a meeting with a customer group or an invitation to create future scenarios).
3. A sufficiently large number of organizational members become aware of the new situation and bring to conscious awareness the collective meaning that is dissonant with it.
4. When a sufficient number of members have brought the collective meaning to conscious awareness, their meaning structures again become part of the accessible meaning in the organization and are again available to be addressed.
5. Through dialogue, members search their accessible meaning structures and private meaning structures in an effort to reduce the dissonance.
6. Members may also seek new information external to the organization to reduce the dissonance.
7. Through dialogue, the existing collective meaning structures are altered or new meaning structures are constructed that take into account the new information and thus are more useful.
8. When a critical mass of individuals have altered their meaning structures the new meaning structures become collective.
9. Over time, the new meaning structures may again become tacit.

The negative effects of collective meaning structures are so familiar to organizations and so pervasive that when new ideas are wanted it has become customary to segregate the hoped for innovators geographically so that organizational members do not reinforce each other's collective meaning structures. Likewise, when new forms of work process are initiated it is common to try them in greenfield sites rather than attempting to change the collective meaning structures of members at an existing site.

In large organizations or organizations in which distinct cultures exist in different sections there may, in fact, be fewer meaning structures which are collective. More accurately, there may be collective meaning structures in differing

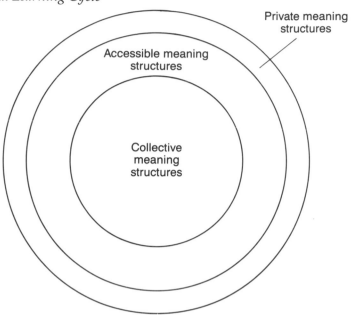

Figure 3.3   Meaning structures in tradition-bound organizations.

sections of the organization but organizational members may hold few collective meaning structures that are consistent across the total organization.

Organizations may vary considerably in the ratio of collective, accessible and private meaning. Organizations which have the greatest capacity for learning are those in which the accessible meaning is the most prominent. In organizations like those depicted in Fig. 3.3, which are tradition-bound, little organizational learning occurs. The organization may still function successfully, particularly if it is in a stable environment, but the organization will have little capacity for self-transformation. Likewise, organizations in which most meaning is held privately, like the organization depicted in Fig. 3.4, have little capacity for organizational learning. There may, of course, be a great deal of individual learning occurring in such organizations. Organizational members may be attending classes, reading journals, getting advanced degrees etc. – it is just that such learning does not affect the way the organization functions because the meaning that organizational members gain from the learning is not available to others. We could construct yet other pictures of organizations in which the ratio of private, accessible and collective meaning varies and postulate why such variance occurs.

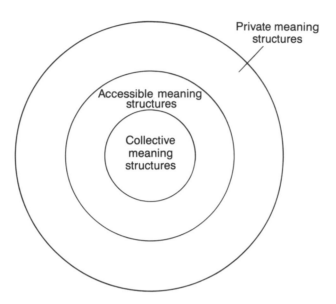

Figure 3.4   Meaning structures in organizations of independent workers.

Organizational learning is strengthened by making more of individuals' private meaning structures accessible so that they can influence other members, as well as by making the collective meaning structures accessible so that they can be tested and altered. In either situation the need is to make the meaning structures accessible to others so they can be exchanged and examined. To accomplish that requires systematic processes, a culture that supports collective learning, and skills and knowledge that facilitate collective learning. It is to these issues that we turn in the next chapters.

References

Argyris, C. and Schon, D. A. (1978). *Organizational Learning: A Theory of Action Perspective*. Reading MA: Addison-Wesley.

Louis, M. R. and Sutton, R. I. (1991). Switching cognitive gears: From habits of mind to active thinking. *Human Relations*, **44** (1), 55–76.

McClellan, J. (1983). *Toward a general model of collective learning: A critique of existing models of specific social systems and a sketch of a model for social systems in general*. Unpublished dissertation, University of Massachusetts.

Weisbord, M. R. and 35 International Coauthors (1992). *Discovering Common Ground*. San Francisco: Berrett-Koehler.

4 The Organizational Learning Cycle

For organizational learning to occur it is not enough simply to encourage organizational members to exchange their accessible meaning structures with each other – the organization must actively facilitate collective learning. In this chapter I describe an organizational learning cycle that involves four steps:

1. Widespread generation of information.
2. Integration of new/local information into the organizational context.
3. Collective interpretation of information.
4. Having authority to take responsible action based on the interpreted meaning.

Four Steps

The four steps are circular in that the fourth step, having authority to take responsible action on the interpreted meaning, generates yet more information and begins the cycle again (see Fig. 4.1)

The steps of generating, integrating, interpreting and acting on information are not new to organizations. However, organizations typically carry out these steps in ways that severely limit organizational learning. Typically, a different part of the organization conducts each step. For example, the Marketing department often assumes responsibility for collecting external information, Research and Development is responsible for generating new ideas and products, MIS is tasked with the distribution of information within the organization, the interpretation of information is accomplished by top management, and those who take action based on the interpretation are often at lower levels in the organization far removed from those who made the interpretation. When the steps of the organizational learning cycle

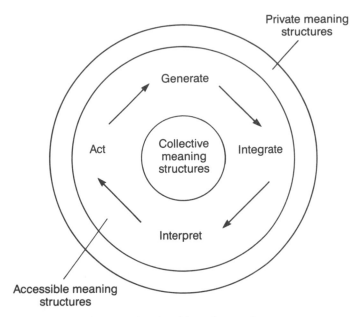

Figure 4.1   The organizational learning cycle.

are disconnected, collective learning is lost. If we want organizational learning to occur, then we must make drastic changes in the way these four steps are undertaken as well as who accomplishes them. The organizational members who generate the data will need to be involved in the interpretation, but not without understanding the context in which it exists, which means having a more complete picture of the organization. The organizational members who make the interpretation need also to be the ones to act on it in order to learn the extent to which their interpretation made sense and what additional data are needed to make a better interpretation.

It may be helpful to relate the organizational learning cycle to Kolb's (1984) experiential learning cycle which I summarized in Chapter 2. For organizational learning to occur, each member of the organization must still engage in all the steps of the experiential learning cycle. But a great deal more must transpire to create collective, rather than just individual, learning. Figure 4.2 relates the steps in the organizational learning cycle to the experiential learning cycle.

In Kolb's model the individual engages in a concrete experience; at the collective level it is necessary that all organizational members engage in the practices that gather information from the external environment (customers, suppliers, conferences) and that likewise all engage in work-related experiments that produce new information. In Kolb's

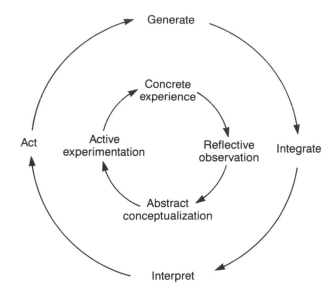

Figure 4.2   The organizational learning cycle and the experiential learning cycle.

model the second step is reflective observation: the individual reflects on an experience, recalling what was notable, or, to use the language of Chapter 2, what was different. Again, at the collective level, the task is more complex: everyone needs all of the information everyone else has. The task is one of integrating newly generated information into the organizational context. The third step in Kolb's model is abstract conceptualization. The individual draws conclusions about the experience, but in organizational learning the task of interpreting information is a collective one. Organizational members come to the task with different perspectives, and therefore different ways of interpreting the information. Those differences are critical to the organizational learning process: without difference learning does not occur. Finally, in Kolb's model the individual is able to test out the conclusions that he or she has reached through active experimentation. Likewise, for collective learning, organizational members must act on the collective interpretation they have made. Action serves both to test the interpretation and to generate new information to continue the learning.

Before describing these four steps in detail, I want to provide three case examples of organizational learning. These examples illustrate the variety of ways organizations have implemented the basic steps of the organizational learning cycle. All of these organizations are self-proclaimed learning organizations and have been extensively written about in the literature as such.

However, I want to share with the reader the hesitancy I have about offering case examples. One difficulty is how to offer illustrations without implying a causal relationship. All of these organizations are successful, or were at the time of their reports; however, we have no way of knowing the extent to which that success is a result of the organizational learning processes that they have implemented. These organizations were involved in many other initiatives at the same time as they were implementing processes related to learning, and those initiatives or even just the general circumstances at the time may well have affected their performance as much as the learning processes themselves. Moreover, it is conceivable that an organization could implement all of the steps of the organizational learning cycle and still fail because the organization simply had a poor product or service, the market was too fragmented, the organization was under capitalized, or because of a hundred other factors unrelated to organizational learning.

Even if we wanted to make a claim about the relationship between organizational learning and success, we would first have to agree upon what success was. The success of the World Health Organization, one of the examples I offer, is of a considerably different nature from the success of another example, Chaparral Steel. The definition of organizational learning that I offered earlier (the intentional use of learning processes at the individual, group and system level to continuously transform the organization in a direction that is increasingly satisfying to its stakeholders) does not necessarily imply success.

A second concern I have in offering case examples is that they are primarily, although not exclusively, taken from the organizational literature. There is a tendency for journal articles to be promotional; most tend to build a case for the success of the organization as well as for the processes that were used to achieve that success. We rarely get a balanced picture that incorporates a sense of the problems that the organization had in implementing the processes or any new problems that might have resulted from the implementation. We also lack understanding of the tacit knowledge that was necessary to the implementation of these processes: most of what we read about are explicit actions.

Finally, I would be violating the principles I have articulated in this book if I were to say, 'Here is how to do it: simply copy WHO or do it the way Chaparral or Johnsonville

Foods does'. I believe each organization must use its own learning capacity to invent the specific processes it needs for organizational learning.

Having made so many caveats the reader may wonder why the case examples are here at all. They are here because I believe they are useful in illustrating the wide variety of ways the steps of the organizational learning cycle might be implemented. I have selected the examples on the basis of variety, although all of the examples are in relatively small organizations, particularly compared with most *Fortune 500* companies. The variety lends credence to the idea that we can learn for ourselves the way to implement the basic principles. I would hope the cases would be viewed as a source of ideas, but not as answers.

In the end, perhaps, the examples are most useful in helping us see that something is possible. It is always difficult to put our energies into learning how to do something until we believe it can be done.

Chaparral Steel

Chaparral Steel is a minimill in Midlothian, Texas. It is the tenth largest US steel producer, with sales over $400 million. Chaparral has taken as its goal to lead the world in the low-cost, safe production of high-quality steel. Much of the success of Chaparral can be attributed to a culture that is focused on learning. It is, however, important to place that culture within the context of the industry.

In the 1950s the US steel industry contained a small number of fully integrated steel manufacturers. Firms typically owned iron and coal mines, railroads to transport the raw materials to the mills, and trucks to deliver the finished products to the customers. There was little or no foreign competition and the major competitive factor among US companies was price, with little differentiation in type of product. Under these circumstances US steel makers devoted little effort to research and development or even to plant modernization. When US labour costs rose in the 1970s, foreign competitors, who had rebuilt their mills with the latest technology after the Second World War, proved too much for these large integrated mills, many of which declared bankruptcy.

Minimills began to emerge in the mid-1970s. They had approximately 6 per cent of the market in 1975, and that had increased to 26 per cent by 1990. The minimills are technology driven, mostly non-unionized and are focused on quality speciality products, such as reinforcing bars, beams, angles and large rounds. Where the larger mills were fully integrated, the minimills recycled scrap. When Chaparral began production of steel in 1975 there were fewer than a dozen minimills; by the mid-1980s there were 60. Chaparral's most challenging competition has come from Third World companies that pay employees as little as $2.30 an hour. In order to compete in this fast growing market Chaparral has had to steadily reduce the number of hours needed to produce a ton of steel. Currently Chaparral produces steel at 1.3 hours per ton, against an industry average of 10 hours per ton. The steel business has traditionally been labour-intensive, capital-intensive and energy-intensive. To compete, Chaparral needed to enlist the aid of its employees to design those elements out of the production process.

Chaparral considers itself a 'Learning Lab' and has some straightforward principles that it uses to reach its competitive goals: (1) owning the problem and solving it, (2) garnering and integrating knowledge, and (3) challenging the *status quo*. The principles are ones that many organizations strive to put into place. Chaparral has been able to make them work, in part, because they are accomplished within a culture based on the belief that human nature is inherently good, energetic, creative and trustworthy. There is an overriding belief in the power of the human mind to invent and create. Chaparral has had the advantage of being a greenfield site and thus hiring employees with the principles and beliefs in mind. In fact, an early employment policy was to avoid potential staff who had worked in the steel industry and thus might have learned practices antithetical to the ones Chaparral was using.

Owning the Problem and Solving it

Because of an unambiguous mission which is translatable into operational objectives, employees are given discretion both to identify and to solve problems independently. The norm is: if you have a good idea, act on it. This means that 90 per cent of the problems never make it to a morning meeting but are solved on the spot, often by spontaneous meetings of those involved in the problem. The downside of this flexibility is that engineers, who might have a better way to address problems, are often not called.

The willingness to own and solve problems is fostered by an egalitarianism. There are no status symbols like assigned parking or separate dining areas at Chaparral. Operators are not assigned to shifts by seniority; rather everyone rotates onto night shift, ensuring that knowledge is spread across shifts. There are no hourly wage earners, everyone is paid a salary, and of course no time clocks. There is a 'no fault' approach to sickness and absenteeism and no reporting structure to track individual employees' absenteeism, yet overall employee absenteeism is less than 1 per cent. Bonus systems are linked to company profits, 8½ per cent of the gross profit before taxes. Ninety-three per cent of employees are stockholders. Chaparral is a flat organization with only two levels between the CEO and the operators in the mill.

Garnering and Integrating Knowledge

This principle is operationalized by employees every day, in every project, adding to the knowledge resources. Employees use the steel process itself as an analogy to talk about an 'unimpeded flow of information' rather than 'batch-processed information'. This flow is aided by Chaparral's size, which is deliberately held to under a thousand employees. The building structure is also deliberately designed to enhance the flow of information: for example, the locker room is located in the headquarters building so employees pass through at least twice a day. The building design provides many opportunities for members to have accidental and frequent meetings. Work is also structured with the objective of disseminating knowledge. For example, the initial team on a new process is subsequently, deliberately dispersed among the rest of the crews to diffuse the knowledge.

There is an emphasis on multi-skilling and multi-functioning. For example, everyone is considered a salesperson and has a business card to use with customers. Security guards do data entry while on night duty. Fork-lift operators do their own routine maintenance. Janitors are able to enter customer orders into the system. Sales, billing, credit and shipping are all housed under the same roof and employees are cross-trained to be able to perform each other's functions. If a customer calls shipping, that person can also answer billing or credit questions. Likewise there are few staff positions: typical staff functions such as hiring, safety, training and MIS reside within line departments. This multi-functioning not only makes the organization more flexible, it also reduces territorial possessiveness over information. The pay structure rewards the accumulation of skills as well as performance.

A critical element for learning is the integration of research and development with production; development takes place on the floor. There is no separate R&D department: the lab is the plant. There are, at times, miniature models of equipment on the factory floor that allow workers to try out new processes or procedures before engaging the expensive full-size equipment. This facilitates 'what if' thinking that might not even be considered without this 'thinking aid'. The people who make the steel are responsible for keeping their process on the leading edge of technology. All employees consider themselves to be part of research and development. For example, two maintenance workers invented a machine for strapping bundles of steel rods together that reduced the cost from $250 000 to $60 000 and was faster and more flexible.

The focus on innovation goes beyond the factory floor. For example, on a Monday morning in Los Angeles a customer suggested to a Chaparral representative that he would buy more steel if minor modifications were made in the size and shape of a particular product. On Monday afternoon those changes were discussed in a production meeting at the plant in Midlothian, Texas. A decision was made to meet the customer's specifications and by Wednesday the new product was being produced. Within two weeks of the initial request the product was being delivered.

Winning as a company takes precedence over individual ownership of ideas. The belief is that ideas go through a gestation period where lots of people figure out how to make the idea work. Individuals are not singled out for praise because of the belief that if individuals are singled out they will begin to protect good ideas. The result is that Chaparral employees are often unable to identify the source of production innovation – the reward for having ideas is getting to carry them out. But neither are they singled out for blame. There is an absence of punitive actions following failures. Mistakes are considered a normal part of risk taking and as important learning opportunities.

Chaparral invests heavily in training of all kinds but places particular emphasis on their apprenticeship programme which was developed in collaboration with the US Department of Labor's Bureau of Apprenticeship and Training. The apprenticeship programme is a three and a half year programme that allows employees to reach the level of senior operator after 7280 hours of on-the-job training and formal schooling. Selected foremen rotate in from the floor to teach the formal part of the programme, teaching such topics as metallurgy, basic mechanical maintenance, basic engineering, and ladder logic programming. The philosophy of the programme is stated as 'It is the intent of Chaparral Steel to provide the broadest possible growth experience for every person employed by the company. We believe that the company grows in excellence in direct proportion to the growth of its people' (Chaparral Steel, 1987, p. 10). Ninety per cent of employees participate in some form of training programme. Much of the learning is conducted on the job or through cross-training, but even so, employees average four hours per week in a classroom. This figure is in sharp contrast to national statistics which reveal that training is primarily offered to managers, with nationally less than 30% of line workers receiving job training. There is a sabbatical plan for front-line supervisors at Chaparral. Chaparral discovered that supervisors typically stay engaged for about three years and then tend to get bored with the job. Supervisors are sent on sabbatical to do special projects and while they are gone others are put in place as substitutes. Chaparral calls this 'vice-ing'. Substitutes often break the productivity records of absent supervisors, giving them something to shoot for when they return. Sabbatical projects might include visiting other steel mills, spending time with customers, or looking into new equipment or programmes under consideration.

Challenging the
'Status Quo'

Chaparral selects employees for their desire to challenge their own and others' thinking. They look for innovators and for individuals with a positive attitude toward learning. Gordon Forward, president and CEO, says, 'We're looking for managers who can do more than just run the company. They must improve it. If all we wanted to do was run this plant, we could get rid of the kind of people we have – the kind who never leave it alone' (Chaparral Steel, 1987, p. 15). Typically eight applicants are interviewed for each one granted a second interview, which takes place in the prospective department. The second interview lasts most of a day and is held not only with the immediate supervisor but with members of the work group.

Large and small experiments are continually being con-ducted. Line managers can authorize tens of thousands of dollars for experiments without higher authority. An example of this experimentation is setting goals beyond current production capabilities. Howard Duff, General Manager, in explaining why a particular product was being developed says, 'We decided on the twenty-four-inch because we wanted to explore the most technically challenging product. Because there may be some idiosyncrasies about the process that we need to learn . . . ' (Leonard-Barton, 1992, p. 25).

Employees scan the world for technical expertise that others have created. They benchmark against best-of-class companies, even from totally different industries. Believing that by the time they hear about an innovation at a conference it will be too late, Chaparral has developed an extensive network to gain early access to new ideas. Multi-level teams visit universities, maintain long-term relation-ships with suppliers, and visit competitors. Chaparral invests heavily in employee travel for benchmarking or to investigate a new technology. Teams have been sent to Japan, Sweden and West Germany to investigate what other industries have to offer. Knowledge does not need to filter down because the people who gather the information are the same people who will use it.

While functioning like a learning laboratory Chaparral has set world records for monthly tonnage. By 1984 the company was listed in *Fortune* as one of the ten best-managed factories in the US. Chaparral put out 1000 tons of steel per worker-year in 1989, compared with the US average of 350 tons and the Japanese average of 600 tons. Chaparral's profit margin is 11 per cent of sales compared with an industry average of 6 per cent. Employee turnover is less than 2 per cent per quarter compared with the 10 per cent US manufacturing average. Among the indicators of which Chaparral is most proud is being the only US steelmaker to be awarded the Japanese Industrial Standard certification in 1989.

In Fig. 4.3 I have extrapolated some of the learning initiatives at Chaparral Steel and placed them within the four steps of the organizational learning cycle. In so doing it is evident that some of what Chaparral has been involved in is not represented in the figure. Yet it is equally clear that Chaparral is heavily investing in each of the steps of the organizational learning cycle.

In the first step, widespread generation of information, Chaparral has certainly excelled. There are concerted efforts to involve every member of the organization in collecting information to bring into the organization: the field visits made by multi-functional teams and the intentional fostering of networks to gain early access to new technology. Even the sabbatical plan for supervisors seems designed to give employees first-hand experience.

Chaparral has done an equally good job of involving everyone in the generation of new internal information. Thinking of the factory floor as a Learning Lab epitomizes that attitude. The resource allocation of $10 000 for experi-mentation, the integration of R&D and production, and hiring based on learning potential all are effective ways to implement the generation of new information.

The second step of the organizational learning cycle, integrating new/local information into the organizational

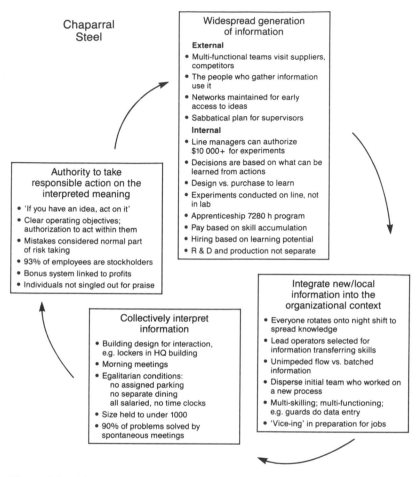

Figure 4.3   The organizational learning cycle for Chaparral Steel.

context, is again accomplished by a number of processes: the multi-skilling and multi-functioning that occurs, the dispersal of initial teams so that their new knowledge is spread and the rotating shifts. Factory workers who consider themselves salespersons must certainly have a broader understanding of the organization into which to position the information they are generating. Perhaps most impressive is the metaphor of an unimpeded flow of information.

The third step, collectively interpreting information, is facilitated by the size of Chaparral, which is deliberately held to under 1000 people, and by the physical design of space that encourages frequent interaction. The egalitarian conditions, which include such things as all salaried employees, no time clocks and no assigned parking spaces, create a climate in which employees are more likely to challenge and question. Much of the interpretation of information at Chaparral appears to go on in spontaneous meetings that occur when a problem arises.

The fourth step, authority to take responsible action on the interpreted meaning, grows out of the third step: those who meet to solve the problem then act on the interpretation they have made. The reward system of Chaparral facilitates action by the bonus system linked to profits and by the stockholder plan. There appears to be a thoughtful norm about not singling individuals out for praise in a way that would discourage joint ownership of problems and solutions.

World Health Organization

In 1966 the World Health Organization (WHO) established a goal to rid the Earth of smallpox. Before its eradication 10 million people a year were inflicted with the disease. Smallpox spreads by minute droplets that are discharged from the mouth and nose of infected victims. About 10–15 days after inhaling the virus the infected person becomes sick with a high fever and flu-like symptoms. A rash appears on the face and within a day or two spreads over the entire body. The pimple-like papules become enlarged and by the fifth day are filled with pus. By the tenth day scabs begin to form, and then fall off by the third week, leaving pitted scars. Once smallpox has been contracted there is no effective treatment. Twenty to forty per cent of those infected die, and those recovering are left scarred and sometimes blind. The disease can be transmitted from the time the rash appears to the time the scabs drop off, a period of about four weeks.

The decision to wage the 1966 campaign was not simply a response to new technology. A smallpox vaccine had been available for several decades before. In fact, a similar campaign, although not carried out, had been proposed to the League of Nations as early as 1926. By 1966 the widespread use of the vaccine in North America and Western Europe had virtually eliminated smallpox from those areas, except for occasional outbreaks resulting from importation.

The guiding strategy of the WHO for the elimination of smallpox was to conduct mass vaccination in the 30 countries where smallpox was epidemic. In 1966 past experience in epidemiology overwhelmingly indicated that the most successful strategy was surveillance and control. The WHO, however, chose mass vaccination, a strategy that involves immunizing 80 per cent of the population on the supposition that smallpox would then decline more or less automatically. The choice of mass vaccination over surveillance and control was influenced by the effectiveness of a test conducted in 1963 on the island of Tonga. Through hindsight it is possible to see that a strategy that was effective in an isolated and remote location might not be transferable to more contiguous areas; however, at the time the mass vaccination strategy appeared well based and sound.

The mass vaccination strategy was employed from the initiation of the campaign until it finally came into question following a smallpox outbreak in eastern Nigeria, an area where 90 per cent of the population had already been vaccinated. Delay in the delivery of supplies to the Nigerian area necessitated a temporary change in strategy. With only a limited amount of vaccine available, new smallpox cases were searched out and vaccinations were given in the immediate geographical area surrounding each case. By the time the mass-campaign supplies arrived a few months later, there were no detectable cases in eastern Nigeria. The containment strategy had worked.

As a result of the Nigeria experience and several other similar experiences, the worldwide strategy was changed to surveillance–containment. This strategy, which was whimsically called '"The Bank Robber Theory" – go where the money is', involved discovering new outbreaks before the smallpox had time to spread, then vaccinating the victims' families, neighbours, and then the village, in an ever-widening circle until no more cases occurred. Using this strategy it was discovered that smallpox could be contained even when only 50 per cent of the population was vaccinated. Ultimately, the surveillance and containment strategy proved itself successful in the worldwide campaign. It is to the credit of the WHO that rather than defending its initial strategy, the organization was able to interpret the data and reframe the strategy.

Over time the WHO came to realize that its initial estimates of the amount of vaccine needed, the incident rate and the morbidity rate, to name only a few of the factors, were woefully inaccurate and underestimated, in some cases by a factor of 40. Thus, the problem, as initially defined, was inaccurate. It was the organization's ability to learn that permitted the WHO to redefine problems repeatedly and thereby make the major shifts in strategy necessary to combat the disease.

The method of vaccination is another example of change in strategy. Traditionally smallpox vaccination had been given by the scratch method, in which a drop of vaccine was placed on the skin and then scratched into the superficial layers. The

WHO decided to use the jet injector, which had recently been invented by the US military. The jet injector was an improvement both because it used less vaccine and because it could provide a standard dosage and could therefore be used by relatively untrained personnel. Perhaps most influential in this decision was that the jet injector represented the latest technology – it was capable of handling up to 1000 vaccinations an hour. Over time, fieldworkers realized that speed had little advantage in a campaign that was more likely to advance from house to house or occur while standing by the town well. The jet injector also presented ongoing problems of cost and maintenance. The bifurcated needle which eventually replaced it was almost primitive by contrast. It allowed a single drop of vaccine to flow between two needles placed like the tines of a fork. The bifurcated needle could be boiled or flamed with a match over 200 times without dulling. Thus it was more field-worthy, if less high-tech. By 1969 the bifurcated needle was being used worldwide. Again WHO was able to learn through its field experience rather than defend its original choice.

Early on, WHO recognized the need to learn constantly from the fieldworkers' experience and to adapt and change accordingly. Although policies were established centrally, control resided at the local level. Thus, fieldworkers were able to alter their vaccination processes in keeping with the local culture. In locations where tattooing was used to ward off witchcraft, the vaccination scar became a part of that custom. In some areas midwives were used to encourage vaccination, in others the scar was a sign of the independence of that country, in others radio was used as a major tool, and in yet others, nomads were vaccinated when they arrived at the public water-hole. This variation was systematically recorded and religiously made available to other fieldworkers. Every two to three weeks a summary of the status of the programme with findings and new approaches appeared in WHO's *Weekly Epidemiological Record*. Special papers on operational methods and results of research appeared with equal frequency. Requests for help from the field were treated by the central office with absolute priority and were given immediate response. In addition to yearly regional meetings, all headquarters staff and regional advisors were expected to spend at least one third of their time in the field, visiting each country at least once and preferably twice a year.

The variation in practice and the emphasis on collecting and sharing findings allowed WHO to innovate and learn continuously. The organization learned that even the most longstanding techniques should be questioned. For example, through analysis of the data it was discovered that the time honoured technique of swabbing the vaccination site made no significant difference in bacterial infection; thus costly supplies were eliminated and time was reduced. Through close analysis of the data it was learned that adult women rarely contracted smallpox and thus did not need to be vaccinated; likewise, 95 per cent of the cases occurred in people who had never been vaccinated, so revaccination could be eliminated.

These findings were possible because of the attention WHO gave to the collection of data and perhaps even more because of the type of data WHO choose to collect. It would have advantaged WHO politically to track the number of vaccinations given and the number of areas which were free from smallpox. WHO chose, however, to track trends in the *incidence* of smallpox. Although those data frequently proved embarrassing both to WHO and to the countries in which the cases were reported, it allowed WHO to learn in a way that would not have been possible from data that was more sensitive to public relations. Negative as well as positive results were widely publicized. All data were scrutinized for age, sex, vaccination status and geographic distribution of cases so that use of resources could be maximized.

Considerable attention was given to improving reporting. In some countries a reward was offered to the first person in an area who reported an undiscovered outbreak to authorities. The rewards were large, sometimes equivalent to one month's income for poor villagers. A manual was produced detailing the philosophy of surveillance and outlining methods for improving case detection and notification. A major breakthrough in reporting occurred when each local unit began to be visited regularly by a mobile surveillance team who provided instruction and assistance. The fact that someone was actively and visibly concerned with receiving reports and then acted on those reports encouraged increased reporting.

In 1975, H. Mahler, then Director-General of the WHO said, 'It is the beginning of the end for smallpox, which can never return to ravage the earth as in centuries past. But it is also the beginning of a new era for WHO, which – having shown what can be done to eliminate disease when all nations join together in a unified, coordinated effort – can now attack more effectively the multitude of other major health problems still confronting us' (Mahler, 1975, p. 3).

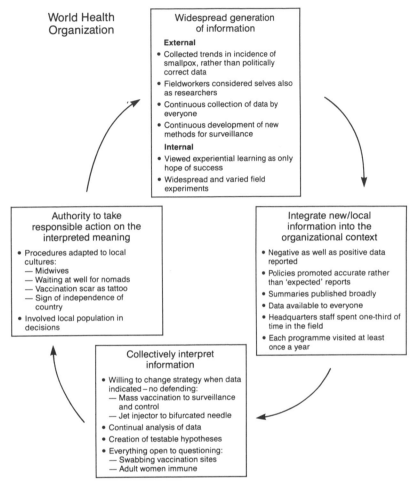

Figure 4.4 The organizational learning cycle for the World Health Organization.

Thus the organizational learning that WHO accomplished not only eradicated smallpox, it resulted in improved national reporting systems for communicable diseases, better techniques for immunization, and more sophisticated communicable disease control services.

The eradication of smallpox was the first global eradication of a major disease. The last case of smallpox occurred in Somalia in 1977.

Figure 4.4 places the initiatives of the World Health Organization within the organizational learning cycle. The first step, the widespread generation of information, was strongly supported by WHO both internally and externally. In particular, the choice of the type of data to collect was significant. Everyone involved in the campaign seemed to feel a responsibility to collect the data that was key to WHO's learning. Like Chaparral, WHO was able to select its employees with learning in mind. Fieldworkers constantly experimented with new processes and techniques. They saw themselves as researchers, not just as dispensers of vaccine.

The second step of the organizational learning cycle, integrating new/local information into the organizational context, reflected a dedication to full and open disclosure of all information. This was accomplished not only through the many reports that were widely circulated, but also by the many field visits of headquarters staff. Fieldworkers had available to them everything that was going on everywhere else: both what was working and what was failing.

The third step, collectively interpreting information, reflects the careful analysis of both statistical and anecdotal data, which was ongoing. The norm of considering everything open to question, even such long-standing traditions as swabbing vaccination sites, served WHO well.

The fourth step, authority to take responsible action on the interpreted meaning, was where WHO excelled. The fieldworkers had authority to act on what they were learning from the data. They were able to vary their practice by local conditions and to involve the local population in those decisions. Control at the local level was not only a necessity to accomplish the task, but also proved a way to enhance the learning. WHO provides an excellent example of how responsible action can lead to the generation of new information.

Johnsonville Foods

Johnsonville Foods was started in 1945 as a sausage company by the Stayer family in a small town in Wisconsin, Johnsonville. In 1968, when the Stayers' son, Ralph, returned from Yale, the sausage company employed 12 people. By 1980, Johnsonville Foods was a very profitable $15 million turnover company that sold its sausage in five states and employed about 200 people.

In the early 1980s Ralph Stayer, now CEO, decided that the organization needed to change. It was profitable and still growing at a rate of 20 per cent annually, but it concerned Stayer that employees did not seem to care: they seemed bored and uninterested in their own performance. They made mistakes, that, while not deliberate, reflected a lack of responsibility – things like driving the prongs of a forklift through a newly built wall, adding the wrong seasonings to a sausage mix, or spraying a batch of sausage with water while cleaning the area. On the other hand he noticed that employees were leading vital lives outside of the organization as active community members involved in scouting and other responsible positions. It worried Stayer that they did not bring this same energy to their jobs.

Stayer was also concerned about competition, both regionally and nationally. National competitors were certainly capable of out-promoting and underpricing a small company like Johnsonville Foods. The regional competitors, of which there were several, could potentially provide better service to customers. Given the uninterested attitude of Johnsonville employees it was difficult to see how the company could survive any serious competitive challenge.

Stayer first looked to the management literature for answers. Finding none that seemed suited to his situation, he determined that he would have to come up with the answers on his own; after all, he concluded, he had, by his own management style, created the situation in which employees were uninterested – he would have to fix it as well.

Stayer's early efforts were to increase communication. He held what came to be known as 4:1s because he often met groups of four people to discuss what they wanted the organization to become. Later the 4:1s became fireside chats that involved 20–25 people. The CEO and other top administrators would articulate their vision for change and they would listen to the concerns of the employees. During this time Stayer's intent was to construct a company goal and then to motivate others to commit to it. What Stayer found over time was that this process did not work: nothing much changed. Stayer came to believe that he had little direct control over the performance of those who reported to him.

The answer, as he began to conceive it, was to create an organization in which people were responsible for their own performance. The metaphor he conceived was a flock of geese on the wing. The geese, he surmised, have a common goal. Each takes turns leading, and most importantly, each of the geese is responsible for its own performance.

People becoming responsible for their own performance, Stayer believed, would take a fundamental shift in the mind set of everyone, including himself. In several journal articles Stayer has chronicled his own struggle to give up power (Stayer, 1990; Brokaw and Hartman, 1990). He came to believe that he had to change, a process he found difficult but rewarding. Responsibility meant that employees needed to be the owners of the problems, which included the power to make decisions related to the problems as well as having all of the information necessary to make the decisions. As an example of that responsibility, prior to the changeover the senior management team met several times a week to evaluate the product; they checked it for taste, colour and texture. As employees assumed more responsibility, the employees themselves did the tasting, but also were given the responsibility to make the changes necessary to improve what went wrong. Employees began to ask for more information on customer reaction, costs, efficiency and yield – data they needed to make the decisions. Information systems had to be redesigned to give them what they needed when they needed it. Increasingly, the information was collected, generated and used by employees themselves with no intermediaries to control the flow. For example, complaint letters from customers began going directly to the line, to address and when necessary to respond to customers. Stayer notes 'There is a lot of talk about making people feel important. I don't agree with that. I think we have to make people *be* important – and know it' (Brokaw and Hartman, 1990, p. 50).

The changeover was accomplished by making major revisions in four pivotal and interrelated systems of the organization: performance management, information/feedback, reward and people.

Performance Management System

Before the 1980s good performance at Johnsonville was, as in most companies, defined by management. The change was to have those who actually do the work define and measure their own performance. Stayer came to believe that 'the real role of the CEO is to generate productive conversations about what performance ought to look like' (Brokaw and Hartman, 1990, p. 50). Thus the new performance system was to be designed from the customer's perspective. The question members were asked to address was: 'For your specific product or service what does great performance look like to the customer?'. Teams who shared a task went to their customers, whether external or internal, to ask that question and then wrestled with how to get those answers down on paper in a way that identified specific results that were measurable. Management set general parameters for budget and production and members were responsible for meeting the standards they had identified within those parameters. Members were, as well, responsible for measuring their performance, which required changes in the second system, information.

Information System

When the performance standards had been identified by the members who actually did the task, Management Information Systems, whose name was changed to Member Information Systems, was asked by the members for assistance in finding ways to generate real-time measures that would allow them to determine how well they were doing and where the problems were. These measures needed to be in a format that was usable to the members themselves. That system then became the way to get continuous improvement, but was also tied to the third system, rewards.

Reward System

Before the change, Johnsonville gave employees two bonuses a year, one before the busy summer season began and one when it was over, as a reward for their hard work. The bonuses rewarded everyone equally regardless of their performance. Recognizing that the old system did not fit the new mind set, Stayer eliminated the bonuses and in their place outlined a new system based on increased responsibility and performance. The new system, however, proved little better than the former system, because it relied on supervisors to identify good performers, a nearly impossible task when supervisors had become coaches of up to 50 members – supervisors simply did not know enough about each individual's performance to make the new system fair and equitable. The reward system was revised once again, but this time by a team of members themselves. The new system rewarded performers based on individual job performance, performance as a team member and personal growth and development. The system was designed and administered by a volunteer team of line production workers from various departments. Twice a year members share a percentage of the company's profit.

People System

What was required was 'to change the focus of the company from using people to build a great business to using the business to build great people' (Honald, 1991, p. 56). An important way the shift was symbolized was no longer to use the term employee (which the dictionary defines as being used for wages) and instead to refer to everyone in the organization as a member.

The people system involves recruiting the right people, developing them, and retaining them. New members are recruited on the basis of their willingness to learn as well as their performance capability. Members became convinced that performance problems resulted from the poor selection of new employees. They ask to be involved in the selection process as well. Selection procedures were established which line workers were able both to follow and eventually to improve. Line workers gradually took over most of the traditional personnel functions. Current members play a major role in the orientation and training of the new members, under the adage that what you teach you learn twice. However, once orientated and trained, members become responsible for their own development. Human Resource Development, now called Member Development, provides the resources to help members determine what they need and to resource those needs, but the responsibility remains with the members themselves. One resource provided is a development fund that sets aside $100 for each member of the company to spend every year on any development activity he or she chooses, which ranges from buying books to attending industry training. Another programme gives any member the opportunity to spend a day with any other member to get a better idea of what the other member's job entails. An extensive email system allows members to share their successes with each other.

The third element of the people system is retention, the goal of which is to assist members who are performing below standard to improve. It is again managed by the members themselves. Any member who is functioning below acceptable levels is coached by other team members who make a contract with the low-performing employee for improvement. Within a well-defined process, teams monitor, correct and, if necessary, even fire their own members.

The initial emphasis on learning was viewed as negative by some organizational members: they felt that learning was personal and not the company's business. Over time, members began to see the connection between learning and their performance and over 65 per cent of the members became involved in some kind of formal education programme. Learning is seen as the acquisition of facts and knowledge, but also as the questioning of actions and behaviour in ways that improve performance.

One of the lessons from the changeover process in which Stayer engaged was the realization that he could not wait until he had a clear picture of how the new systems would work to make the changes – he had to learn his way through the process. He explains that the process was not neat and orderly. 'There were lots of obstacles and challenges, much backsliding, and myriad false starts and wrong decisions' (Stayer, 1990, p. 79). For example, when teams were created and chose their team leaders, almost immediately those leaders began to act like supervisors – they fell into the familiar roles. Stayer discovered that they needed training in order act differently.

Structural changes were made as well. As teams took over many of the processes, less management was needed. The hierarchy went from six layers to three. Staff positions were eliminated when teams took on the selection, training and evaluating roles. Supervisor jobs disappeared when teams took on operational functions of schedules, performance standards, assignments, budgets and capital improvements. The quality control function changed its focus and became technical support to production people.

One example of the information/responsibility pairing is the decision Johnsonville faced in 1985 about whether to accept an offer from a food-processing company to buy large quantities of product on a regular basis. Johnsonville did not have the capacity to handle the job. Before the changeover, Stayer would have gathered his management team and they would have hammered out the pros and cons and made a strategic decision. What Stayer did in this situation was to call a meeting of the whole organization, giving them all of the information he had and asking them to work in teams to answer three questions; What will it take to make it work? Is it possible to reduce the downside? Do we want to do it? The teams struggled with the questions for almost two weeks, wrestling with the risks, which were considerable, and how they would have to operate to accomplish that much increase in production. In the end the teams almost unanimously decided to take on the new business.

Outcomes

From 1982 to 1990 Johnsonville's return on assets has doubled, sales have increased eight-fold and rejects have been reduced from 5 per cent to less than 0.5 per cent. Since 1982, productivity has increased nearly 300 per cent. Johnsonville Foods is in 45 states with sales of $150 million, 600 employees, and three manufacturing facilities. Some of this improvement should be credited to improved technology, but Johnsonville Food's leaders believe the learning initiative is largely responsible. Stayer says, 'If you issue orders, you're telling people, Don't think; just do. But if you've got 1000 people, you've got 1000 minds. And if you issue orders from the top, you're using only 3 of them, or 2, or one. That's stupid' (Brokaw and Hartman, 1990, p. 50).

Figure 4.5 places the learning processes of Johnsonville Foods in the organizational learning cycle. Of the three cases, Johnsonville Foods is the only one in which a change effort

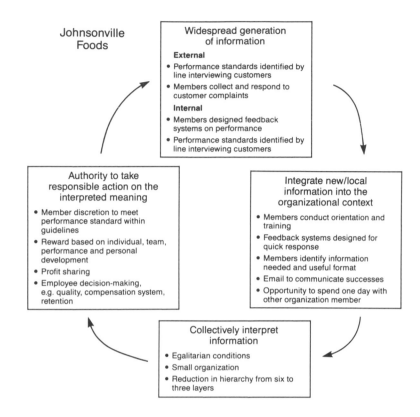

Johnsonville
Foods

**Widespread generation
of information**

External
- Performance standards identified by
  line interviewing customers
- Members collect and respond to
  customer complaints

Internal
- Members designed feedback
  systems on performance
- Performance standards identified by
  line interviewing customers

Authority to take
responsible action on the
interpreted meaning

- Member discretion to meet
  performance standard within
  guidelines
- Reward based on individual, team,
  performance and personal
  development
- Profit sharing
- Employee decision-making,
  e.g. quality, compensation system,
  retention

Integrate new/local
information into the
organizational context

- Members conduct orientation and
  training
- Feedback systems designed for
  quick response
- Members identify information
  needed and useful format
- Email to communicate successes
- Opportunity to spend one day with
  other organization member

Collectively interpret
information

- Egalitarian conditions
- Small organization
- Reduction in hierarchy from six to
  three layers

Figure 4.5   The organizational learning cycle for Johnsonville Foods.

was made: the other two examples had the luxury of selecting personnel and establishing norms with learning in mind. Stayer has helpfully chronicled some of the change process so we are able to understand what worked and what did not.

In the first step of the organizational learning cycle, widespread generation of information, we can see that change played out in the performance standards that did not work until employees themselves got involved by clarifying them with customers. In the second step as well we see the change process: MIS changes from controlling information to a service to members for identifying what information they will need and the form in which it is needed. The third step, collectively interpreting information, as with Chaparral Steel, can be attributed to the size of the organization, which has deliberately been kept small. The process in which the organization engaged to reach the decision to take on the new business is a good example of collective interpretation.

From the description it is clear that this decision was not a matter of a vote, but was a thoughtful interpretation of organization-wide data. The fourth step, authority to take responsible action on the interpreted meaning, was Stayer's original goal. His chronicle makes clear the difficulty of accomplishing that unless the other three steps are in place.

References

Brokaw, L. and Hartman, C. (1990). Managing the journey. *Inc*, November, 45–54.

Chaparral Steel Apprenticeship Program (1987). Midlothian: Chaparral Steel.

Honald, L. (1991). The power of learning at Johnsonville Foods. *Training*, April, 55–8.

Kolb, D. A. (1984). *Experiential Learning*. Englewood Cliffs NJ: Prentice-Hall.

Leonard-Barton, D. (1992). The factory as a learning laboratory. *Sloan Management Review*, Fall, 23–38.

Mahler, H. (1975). Smallpox – point of no return. *World Health*, February/March. pp. 3.

Stayer, R. (1990). How I learned to let my workers lead. *Harvard Business Review*, **68** (6), 66–83.

Background Reading

Douglas, J. H. (1975). Death of a disease. *Science News*, **107** (Feb.), 74–5. World Health Organization.

Dumaine, B. (1992). Chaparral Steel: Unleash workers and cut costs. *Fortune*, **125** (10), 18. (Chaparral Steel.)

Forward, G. E., Beach, D. E., Gray, D. A. and Quick, J. C. (1991). Mentofacturing: a vision for American industrial excellence. *Academy of Management Executive*, **5** (3), 32–44. (Chaparral Steel.)

Henderson, D. A. (1976). The eradication of smallpox. *Scientific American*, **235** (4), 25–33. (World Health Organization.)

Henderson, D. A. (1977). Smallpox shows the way. February/March, 22–7. World Health Organization.

Hopkins, J. W. (1988). The eradication of smallpox: Organizational learning and innovation in international health administration. *The Journal of Developing Areas*, **22**, 321–32. (World Health Organization.)

Kantrow, A. M. (1986). Wide-open management at Chaparral Steel. *Harvard Business Review*, **64** (3), 96–102. (Chaparral Steel.)

Lee, C. (1990). Beyond teamwork. *Training*, **2** (6), 25–32. (Johnsonville Foods.)

Luthans, F. (1991). Conversation with Gordon Forward. *Organizational Dynamics*, **20** (1), 63–72. (Chaparral Steel.)

McKague, A. (1992). 'Learning culture' vital. *Computing Canada*, **18** (3), 11. (Chaparral Steel.)

McManus, G. J. (1992). Beaming with pride. *Iron Age*, 14–17. (Chaparral Steel.)

Quick, J. C. and Gray, D. A. (1989/90). Chaparral Steel Company: Bringing 'world class manufacturing' to steel. *National Productivity Review*, **9** (1), 51–8. (Chaparral Steel.)

5   Theory and Research – The Organizational Learning Cycle

In this chapter I want to add much greater detail to each step of the organizational learning cycle. I have extrapolated some of the elements that are critical from the three case studies and have added some examples from other organizations as well in an attempt to round out the description. I have also provided supporting theory where it is available. Although much less theoretical and empirical research has been done on collective learning than individual learning, there are some findings that can add depth to the anecdotal information provided in the case studies. Figure 5.1 displays the abstracted elements related to each step of the organizational learning cycle.

Step 1 – Widespread Generation of Information

I have used the term 'generate' for this step of the organizational learning cycle to encompass both the collection of external data and the internal development of new ideas, including both process and product. Within external information I include information about customers, suppliers, new technology and economic conditions, to name a few of many possible sources of information. Generating external information requires crossing the organization's boundaries to interact with the world external to the organization. By contrast, internal information is developed through the process of conducting the organization's business and occurs within the boundaries of the organization. It includes analysing successes and mistakes, creating experiments designed to provide new information, and building checkpoints into activities so that the activity can become self correcting.

There is a second operative term in the label of this first step: 'widespread'. I am suggesting that the generation of information needs to be the responsibility of all members of the organization rather than leaving those tasks to specialized functions, such as R&D or customer service.

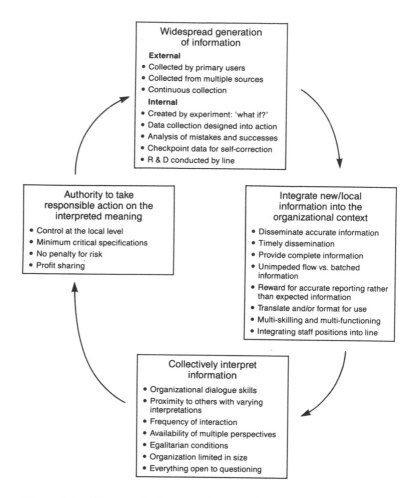

Figure 5.1   Elements in the organizational learning cycle.

External Information   The rationale for shared responsibility was, to some extent, explained in Chapter 2 in discussing the importance of differences for learning. It is not difference itself but the resolution of differences through self-confrontation that is at the heart of learning.

For individual learning, self-confrontation means an individual is able to hold multiple views in his or her mind at one time in order to make sense of them. For organizational learning, self-confrontation means that an individual, as a sub-system of the organization, must be able to confront others who have constructed a different meaning. Likewise, one department must be able to confront another department which has constructed a meaning unique to it. Friedlander

(1984) says, 'Organizational learning occurs at the interfaces between persons, between organizational units, and between the organization and its external environment' (p. 199). As each sub-system interacts with the external environment and then internally with other sub-systems it creates a unique perspective which it then adds to the diversity of ideas and to the diversity of relationships that can be built between those ideas. Diversity of ideas and perspectives is necessary for learning through self-confrontation to occur. We have many societal examples of disparate ideas leading to new learning: the difficulties between sexes have caused a new and more equitable way of being, the difficulties between Japan and the USA has led to improved quality, and the differences between handicapped and non-handicapped has led to a more humane society. Difference, as uncomfortable as it often makes us, leads to learning.

Useful difference within an organization is created when individual members experience the environment in which they function first-hand, rather than through the organized information provided by others. Because all information is influenced and shaped by those who collect it, information that is collected centrally and then distributed has already gone through several layers of filters, which have shaped and to some extent homogenized it.

A basic tenet of systems theory is that heterogeneity produces energy whereas complete homogeneity leads to entropy. A closed system will increasingly develop a homogeneous view; the accessible meaning structures of organizational members will gradually become collective meaning structures and disappear from the organizational dialogue. Diversity is created by opening the organizational boundaries to let in new views.

I am not, however, suggesting a massive duplicative effort where everyone collects every kind of information the organization needs; rather, I am suggesting that information be collected by the primary users of the data. By primary users I mean those who will act on the information. The example of the line workers at Johnsonville Foods directly receiving complaint letters from customers is an illustration of primary users collecting information. There are other unique ways organizations have of involving primary users in the collection of external data. For example, an innovative hospital pays its employees to visit hospitals in other parts of the country while they are on vacation. In these visits what the employee attends to most closely is the function he or she performs back home.

Diversity of meaning is also encouraged by collecting data from multiple sources. Many organizations limit their data collection to standard practices, such as focus groups or customer surveys, but as all three case examples illustrate the informal sources are often as productive as the formal. For example, one construction firm asks employees to note any new construction sites they see on their way to and from work. Another company has a 'competitor alert' file to which managers all contribute on a regular basis. Price-Waterhouse uses a computer program to scan news for any articles on customers. The articles are automatically sent to the partners who are working with those customers.

A final factor related to external information in Fig. 5.1 is continuous collection. The external collection of information is not just to seek a specific answer to an identified problem but serves to identify and raise problems as well. For example, the teams at Chaparral that network to gain access to new technology are looking for opportunity as much as answers – a continuous process.

The continuous collection of information by primary users and through multiple sources is only workable if the second step of the organizational learning cycle is in place. Information about the external environment cannot be closely held but must be made available to others; it must become a part of the organizational context. However, before turning to the second step of the organizational learning cycle it is important to focus on the development of internal information.

Internal Generation of Information

Organizational members in all three of the case examples were heavily involved in generating new information. The factory workers at Chaparral thought of the factory floor as a learning laboratory and designed experiments as a part of carrying out their jobs. The fieldworkers of WHO thought of themselves as researchers. Some experiments are like pilot projects conducted in order to find out if a certain process will work well enough to warrant implementing it more widely. Other experiments are initiated for the purpose of gaining information that will inform related decisions. When Chaparral decided to go with the 24-inch product because it was more 'technically challenging' their purpose was to learn something from the experience that might help them in other areas. They were designing their work in ways that generated information as well as got the job done. 'In any design process questions arise for which objective answers are not available . . . they must be dealt with by incorporation into the design experimental processes for resolving them' (Ackoff, 1981, p. 106).

3M, an organization considered a world-class leader in innovation, reportedly encourages experimentation by allocating 10 per cent of employees' time to working on their own experiments. The example of the maintenance workers who developed a machine to strap bundles of steel rods reflects Chaparral's attitude towards experimenting with new solutions.

When we think about learning from our actions we often mean taking time to reflect at the end of a project or event to consider whether it was a success or failure. That can be a valuable process to help us learn from our actions. We can think of these end-of-project post-mortems as summative evaluation, a kind of report card. There is another type of evaluation, formative, whose purpose is not judgement but course correction. This kind of evaluation happens not at the end of an initiative but during. The analogue might be a self-guided missile which continually takes readings and uses them to correct its course. In one computer manufacturing company, teams start the morning with a 15 minute meeting to review its performance results from the day before. If the results were poor the team works on solving the problem. If the results were good they think through ways to keep the curve moving upward. Revans (1983) has noted: 'Any system that is to learn . . . must regularly receive and interpret inputs about its own outputs' (p. 13). But to accomplish formative evaluation, the plan for data collection must be established up-front. The question consistently asked by organizational members in the three case examples is not only 'What can we do?' but 'What can we learn from what we do?'.

Step 2 – Integrating New/ Local Information Into the Organizational Context

Information that is collected externally and/or generated internally can only be understood within the context of the total organization. The silo phenomenon in organizations is when one part of the organization does not have access to what other parts know (in effect, it cannot learn from them), and it is often decried for this reason. But an equally detrimental effect of the silo phenomenon is the inability of each part to understand its own information because it lacks the context of the whole picture. It would be like closely examining a single piece of a jigsaw puzzle without access to the other pieces. The billing people at Chaparral benefit from the multi-functioning described, not only because they are better able to answer related questions such as those about shipping, but because in knowing about shipping they are better able to answer billing questions.

In order to accomplish the organization's task we must act in concert with each other, and to do that we must share some understanding about what we are trying to accomplish and how we are going about it. Schon (1979) provides an example of shared understanding in his description of a simple craft organization. He first describes the activities of an individual craftsman who is not part of an organization and therefore does all of the many tasks involved in making wooden shovels himself – from selecting logs from which to shape the shovels, to pricing the end product in order to make a profit. Schon suggests that the craftsman carries a picture in his head of the total task and of the relationship of each sub-task to the whole. When the making of shovels is accomplished by a small group of individuals, an organization, instead of a single individual, the sub-tasks are divided among them – but the individuals must still maintain in their heads an image of the whole and the relationship of their parts to it in order to insure that their sub-tasks will fit the whole. For example, the worker who rough cuts the shovels needs to hold an image similar to the one that the worker who fine chisels the shovels holds and so on. Schon explains that 'whereas the individual craftsman controlled the pattern of his own activities, control in the workshop is partly an individual and partly a collective matter' (p. 117).

The distribution of accurate and complete information is a critical element in the integration of new or local information into the organizational context, yet the type and amount of information that is disseminated within organizations is often limited. There are four methods through which the distribution of information is obstructed: message routing, message summarizing, message delay, and message modification (Daft and Huber, 1987). Message routing is the selective distribution of information. Message summarizing is the reduction of the size of the message, for example, reducing large sets of numbers to averages. Message delay relates to when the message is distributed. Message modification is the distortion of meaning. These four methods affect the availability, form and accuracy of information in the organization.

These methods are often used by upper management to control the information employees receive, but they are as frequently used by employees to control the information upper management receives. They are also used to negative effect between sub-units. Examples of such control might include:

- employees modifying negative information that is being reported upward so that it will reflect less negatively on the sender
- management delaying a message to employees until a more favourable time
- a manufacturing department benchmarking a product but giving little thought as to who else in the organization could benefit from the benchmark information
- the organization purchasing an environmental scan for the use of the planning team, but not disseminating the information beyond the level of upper management

The use of message routing, summarizing, delay and modification to control information may be deliberate on the part of any segment of the organization, but such processes are equally likely to be a part of the collective meaning structure of the organization: 'simply the way we do things around here'. Therefore, to resolve the problems related to the distribution of information, the organization must not only create better processes for distribution, it must also question the collective meaning structure that mediates the full and accurate distribution of information.

The elements needed for the second step of the organizational learning cycle are the converse of message routing, summarizing, delay, and modification. All parts of the organization need to provide all other parts with accurate, timely and complete information. The WHO case example illustrates the importance of information: without the courageous choice to report accurate rather than politically sensitive information, the smallpox campaign would have failed. Another example of the dissemination of complete information is the Kao Corporation, where all company information (excepting personnel data) is stored in a single integrated database that is open to any employee regardless of position.

Timeliness of information is illustrated by the Chaparral's metaphor of the unimpeded flow of information rather than batched information. General Electric Aircraft Engines is developing an organization-wide project planning system to both design and store the many projects through which its business is run. This process will integrate the information from projects across the entire system. The consistency in format and documentation will provide the capability to retrieve individual projects or classes of projects which are related by some salient factor.

The case example of the WHO also demonstrates the need for rewarding accurate reporting. The level and quality of local outbreak reports increased when a mobile surveillance team provided personal contact. It is difficult for any of us to send reports down what often seems to be a black hole. Even disseminating information is, to some extent, an interactive process: we need some sense of how our report was received and to what use it was put. In one organization, run largely on a project basis, a brief description of each project is put on the organization's electronic bulletin board. Following the description an impact list is provided, that is, a list of other projects or functional areas that the project members believe will be affected in some way by the project. The description is automatically sent to those on the list, as are weekly updates on the progress of the projects. Frequent response and inquiries from those on the impact list encourage the senders to persist and help them understand more clearly the level of detail that others need as well as the ways in which the information is being put to use.

Tushman and Scanlan (1981) note that specialization within organizations may interfere with information distribution. Specialization increases the efficiency of information processing within a unit, but is a double-edged sword in that it often blocks information from moving across unit boundaries. Idiosyncratic language and local conceptual frameworks work against the distribution of information across specializations. Thus the need for boundary-spanning individuals who are able to understand and translate the information and facilitate shared understanding across organization boundaries. In one highly technical organization, a position of translator or interpreter has been created to bridge the gap between specialisms (materials, design, finance). These boundary-spanning professionals work in the 'cracks' of the organization, translating what one specialism is doing for the benefit of another. In a very different sense, Springfield Remanufacturing Corporation also engages in a kind of translation. It uses a continuous scrolling display on the shop floor to display the organization's performance on numerous indicators. To make sure the indicators have meaning to the viewers, everyone is trained in how to read financial information.

Organizations have found unique ways of integrating information, for example, Johnsonville Foods' policy of giving each employee one day a year to spend with an employee in another department. At Toyota Canada, departments invite employees from other departments into their monthly meetings. They also take staff on tours of the company. Honda requires each manager to exchange jobs for a two-week period with a counterpart in another function. At some General Motors plants performance evaluations include an item on networking that encourages the integration of information. GE has implemented a best practices seminar in which internal best practices are explained in detail and teams from other units have time to plan together about how they might implement the practice in their own unit. In a similar vein, NASA has regularly scheduled success sharing meetings, the purpose of which is to inform others of projects or events that have 'gone right'.

Chaparral Steel provides helpful examples of using multi-functioning and multi-skilling to integrate information, such as the factory workers who have business cards for when they act as sales representatives, the fork-lift operators who do their own routine maintenance, and the janitors who enter customer orders into the system. At both Chaparral Steel and Johnsonville Foods many of the staff functions have been integrated into line responsibilities. At Johnsonville, for example, staff hire, measure employee performance and make disciplinary contracts when necessary.

Step 3 – Collectively Interpreting the Information

Of paramount importance to organizational learning are the processes that are in place to facilitate organizational members collectively interpreting information, the third step of the organizational learning cycle. It is easy to make the mistake of equating giving others information with learning. Leaders often think that if they have widely distributed information, organizational members will 'know it'. As we saw in Chapter 2, receiving information and making meaning from it are very different processes. When an individual is given information, he or she selectively attends to it. Those parts which are selected are examined for patterns and are compared to the meaning the individual has stored in long-term memory. Only when the individual has formed new relationships through this process and again stored those new relationships in long-term memory can we say the individual has learned.

For organizational learning to occur the process is yet more complex. Not only must each individual engage in the sequence just described, each must do so while interacting with other organizational members (who are of course engaged in the same sequence themselves) and out of their interaction the organizational members must form an interpretation of the information. I want to stop short of saying that they must agree upon an interpretation. The goal of collective interpretation is more the reduction in the equivocality of information than reaching consensus. By engaging in collective interpretation each person involved is influenced by the meanings others hold and in turn influences the meanings of others. Each better understands the reasoning and data others are using to arrive at their meaning; thus they understand others' meanings more fully and by comparison, understand their own more fully. Collective interpretation may not develop a definitive answer, but if organizational members fully invest themselves in collective interpretation, they will understand the parameters of the problem more clearly.

The difficult question Johnsonville Foods faced, related to whether to take on the additional work that would stretch its production capacity, is perhaps a useful illustration. There was no textbook answer to the three questions Stayer put to the members of the organization, and even when all the available data pertaining to the issue were laid out, clear-cut answers were still not obvious. It was only through the many days of wrestling with the information that the equivocality was reduced and an interpretation was reached upon which the group agreed to act. Even so, the report was that it was nearly unanimous, not that it was unanimous. We do not all have to be in total agreement in order to act in concert. We do, however, all need to understand fully the reasoning behind the proposed action, and moreover we need the opportunity to influence that reasoning. Collective interpretation provides both opportunities.

In the Johnsonville Foods example the collective interpretation occurred through a relative, formal set of meetings. At Chaparral Steel collective interpretation often occurs spontaneously with a group coming together on the factory floor to deal with a problem that has just arisen. The level of formality is less critical than are the conditions that allow collective interpretation to occur.

However, before turning to those conditions, I want to contrast collective interpretation of information with the more traditional way organizations have attempted to interpret widely dispersed knowledge. Traditionally, someone in a management or supervisory position collects relevant information from subordinates and, armed with the collective information, interprets it and arrives at a conclusion.

Then, based on this interpretation, the supervisor informs subordinates of the actions to take. This is the approach Stayer describes as the way he would have made the production decision before he began the change process. This funnel approach, in which one individual (or sometimes a team) serves as the conduit for the collective information, may be able to take into account some of the information that each individual has to contribute, but it cannot make use of the reasoning they might contribute – and that is a considerable loss to learning. The funnel model is based on assumptions that are antithetical to organizational learning:

1. That information is an accurate representation of reality that, when summed, can provide a 'right' answer, rather than being an interpretation.
2. That it is the information individuals have rather than their meaning-making capability that is most valuable.
3. That learning is one-way rather than a joint activity in which the meaning structures of both or all parties are modified.

Conditions that Enhance Collective Interpretation of Information

We can each name organizations in which we have interacted with our colleagues on a regular basis but where very little collective interpretation occurred. The opportunity to interact is not enough: there must be conditions in place that support collective interpretation. Those conditions include:

- information and expertise that are distributed
- egalitarian values
- the organization's size and physical arrangement support frequent interaction between sub-systems
- processes and skills that facilitate organizational dialogue.

Information and Expertise that are Distributed

Information must be distributed among the individuals engaged in collective interpretation rather than residing in only one or two individuals. If only one or very few organizational members have all of the information related to a subject, collective interpretation is not useful. Step 1 of the organizational learning cycle, in which every individual engages in the collection of external information and in the generation of internal information related to their own function is one way distributed information is achieved. Chaparral sends teams all over the world to look at new technology, talk with competitors and interact with university researchers. These organizational members have first-hand information to bring to organizational interactions.

Having organizational members continually engage in individual training and learning opportunities is a way to achieve distributed expertise. Both Johnsonville Foods and Chaparral Steel place great emphasis on internal training and external educational opportunities. At Chaparral 90 per cent of employees are involved in training, and at Johnsonville 65 per cent – both far exceeding industry averages, particularly for first line employees.

Egalitarian Values

There are three core values that enhance collective interpretation:

- *freedom* to speak openly without fear of punishment or coercion
- *equality*, which must exist for freedom to exist
- *respect*, which must be present for equality to exist

It should not be surprising that freedom and learning are connected. Thomas Jefferson made it clear that without learning that resulted in informed opinion, freedom could not prevail. The converse is also true: without freedom, learning is limited to what others will permit.

'Equality' means that no individual's ideas are more worthy (more right) than any other's by virtue of position or status. The meaning that each individual has constructed is tested against the meanings of others, not against the power or position of others.

'Respect' acknowledges that each individual has constructed meaning structures that make 'sense' to him or her. It acknowledges that there is a logic to their construction that, if we could only grasp it, would allow us to share their world. The other side of respect is humility, the realization that the way I have constructed the world is only my interpretation, which is certain to change. Paulo Freire (1970) says:

> On the other hand, dialogue cannot exist without humility. The naming of the world, through which men constantly re-create the world, cannot be an act of arrogance. Dialogue, as the encounter of men addressed to the common task of learning and acting, is broken if the parties (or one of them) lack humility. How can I dialogue if I always project ignorance onto others and never perceive my own? How can I dialogue if I regard myself as a case apart from other men – mere 'its' in whom I cannot recognize

other 'its'? How can I dialogue if I consider myself a member of the in-group of 'pure' men, the owners of truth and knowledge, for whom all non-members are 'these people' of 'the great unwashed?' . . . . How can I dialogue if I am closed to – and even offended by – the contribution of others? How can I dialogue if I am afraid of being displaced, the mere possibility causing me torment and weakness? Self-sufficiency is incompatible with dialogue. Men who lack humility (or have lost it) . . . cannot be their partners in naming the world (p. 78).

To place collective interpretation at the heart of organizational learning is to affirm the power of the individual mind and equally to affirm the power of the collective mind. It is a Jeffersonian concept that acknowledges the capability of individuals to think for themselves, to manage themselves, to govern themselves. It is an affirmation of democratic ideals over autocratic ideals.

Perhaps one of the reasons so little organizational learning occurs is that the conditions of freedom, equality and respect so rarely exist in organizations. Organizations will not be able to learn effectively until these are manifest.

There is some research evidence that egalitarian values lead to greater organizational learning. Brooks (1993) in a study of collective learning in quality teams says, 'The greatest barrier to collective team learning encountered by the teams . . . was the assumption that some contributions were more valuable than others' (p. 54). In this study it was not the fact that some members knew more than others that limited learning, but the perception of the worth of others' ideas. Conversely, in studies in which organizational members believed others possessed or could construct answers more easily than themselves, they were less willing to do the hard work of learning (Hatano and Inagaki, 1991). I remember Malcolm Knowles, heralded as the father of adult education, as a white-haired octogenarian, saying that one of the most frustrating problems about getting older was that when he spoke to a group, out of respect no one would challenge his ideas, and thus his own learning was severely inhibited. Such inhibitions may occur because of position, perceived expertise, years of experience or a myriad of other factors that cause individuals to experience an imbalance in the relationship.

Hierarchy is a great inhibitor to learning. Friedlander (1983) says, 'Power differences hinder system learning when subordinate components suppress or deny their own resources and expertise, when superior components impose theirs, or when either party distances itself from the other, for example, in order to protect itself' (p. 200). It is not only lower level employees who are likely to learn less when those higher in the hierarchy are present; those individuals who are higher in the hierarchy are also less likely to develop new ideas, because their ideas are not challenged (Hatano and Inagaki, 1991).

Since it is not feasible to eliminate organizational hierarchy, at least in the foreseeable future, organizational members must work at establishing rules and norms which reduce or eliminate its negative impact on collective interpretation. Chaparral works at reducing its effects by such things as all employees being salaried, no special parking and no special dining facilities. Other organizations have developed unique techniques for reducing the learning effects of hierarchy. At Granite Rock, all levels of employee are trained together: there is not the usual segregation by level. At the Corkstown facility of Northern Telecom organizational members have created a 'pink room'. In this room hierarchy does not exist, and colleagues can be forthright in their opinions or ask each other for help with assurance that what is said stays in the pink room.

Size

Collective interpretation is assisted when organizational members have the opportunity for frequent face-to-face interaction. Both Chaparral Steel and Johnsonville Foods have been deliberate about keeping their size small to facilitate that interaction. Although research has not shown how large an organization might be and still be able to engage in collective interpretation of information, it seems obvious that mega-organizations that number in the thousands make many of the conditions listed here unlikely. Chaparral has, as well, designed its building to facilitate interaction. Mars has also used the physical arrangement of its offices to facilitate interaction between levels and departments. The offices are arranged in a pie-shape, with the company officers in the middle. Some organizations use 'caves' and 'coves' to facilitate interaction. Caves are offices only large enough for one person and his or her computer. Coves are common areas with sofas and over-stuffed chairs. They have flip charts and coffee available. If organizational members need to meet with others they must do so in the common area where their colleagues are also meeting. Individual offices behind closed doors would seem to represent a time when we thought of work as an individual task. As we think about work as the function of a team and collective interpretation as a necessity, surely the physical environment of our organizations as well as their size will be modified.

Organizational Dialogue

Organizational dialogue is interaction in a collective setting that results in mutual learning upon which the organization can act. In defining dialogue in this way I am restricting its use to a specific kind of organizational talk; talk that reveals our meaning structures to each other. When that happens we learn and our partners in dialogue learn as well – we achieve a kind of mutual learning. But that is not a common kind of talk in organizations. I am also reserving the term dialogue for a collective setting: two people engaged in a conversation, although important for collective interpretation, would not be organizational dialogue in the sense I am using it here. It may also be important to address the last phrase in the definition, 'upon which the organization can act'. I am, then, not just talking about good communication skills or making another 'feel' heard or feel better about themselves; rather I am implying interaction that is targeted to the organization's business.

To carry on a dialogue the conditions I have described in this section need to be in place. In addition, participants need the skills to:

- provide others with accurate and complete information that bears upon the issue
- confirm others' personal competence when disagreeing with their ideas
- make the reasoning that supports their position explicit; say how they got from the data to the conclusion
- voice the perspective of others
- change position when others offer convincing data and rationale
- regard assertions, their own and others, as hypotheses to be tested
- challenge errors in others' reasoning or data

The use of the term 'skills' for this list may be somewhat misleading. The items on this list might, in fact, seem self-evident to most of us; the reader might say, 'Of course we need all of the available information that pertains to the issue we are considering'. Yet as a researcher who has observed meetings in many organizations, I know that the actual use of these behaviours is rare. It is much more frequent, for example, for participants in a discussion to withhold critical information for fear that it might embarrass themselves or others, to offer their conclusions but not the data on which they were based, and to regard their own position as 'truth' and others' positions as in error.

If the skills appear self-evident yet are in little use, we have to wonder whether there is a skill issue or if it is just that the organizational conditions in which most of us function have made the use of these behaviours hazardous. Drawing on the theory of individual learning described in Chapter 2, I would suggest that we have made not these skills, but their converse, tacit. We have so often withheld our reasoning, refrained from saying what we know others do not want to hear, and held on to our position long after the evidence has proved us wrong, that it is those behaviours that have become automatic. That implies that if we want to employ these skills of dialogue, we may first have to 'unlearn' the tacit ones that are preventing effective dialogue.

In constructing this list of skills for dialogue I have drawn upon the work of several theorists who have written extensively about dialogue: Argyris, Bohm, Mezirow, and Johnson and Johnson.

Provide Others With Accurate and Complete Information that Bears Upon the Issue

The operative phrase in this statement is 'that bears upon the issue'. It is not an argument for total honesty or for saying anything that is on our minds, but rather it speaks to an implicit obligation to a group struggling with an issue to put all relevant information, the good and the bad, on the table so that we all have the information.

Our tendency, however, is to withhold that part of the information that we believe will make us look bad or that we fear will embarrass someone else. Rather than risk that embarrassment we often try to persuade others using substitute arguments and in so doing we add to the equivocality and make the collective interpretation more difficult. Perhaps most importantly we prevent others from correcting us if the information we are so closely guarding is mistaken.

There is a kind of arrogance about withholding the information that we fear will embarrass others. It implies, 'I know what is best for you', removing from others the responsibility for their own actions. Likewise, there is a prejudice suggested in withholding information that we fear will make ourselves look bad. It implies that others will be intolerant of our error, without offering them the opportunity to behave in a tolerant manner. It prejudges others and again prevents us from finding out if we are wrong.

Challenge the Errors in Others' Reasoning or Data

The polite response to hearing what we know to be a mistake in a colleague's reasoning or errors in their facts is to not mention it and to change the subject. Our good intention is to 'save face'. It is, however, the uncertainty provoked by such a challenge which leads to the reorganization of one's meaning structures. Johnson and Johnson (1989, pp. 91–2) describe what happens when we challenge another's ideas:

1. When individuals are presented with a problem or decision, they have an initial conclusion based on categorizing and organizing incomplete information, their limited experiences, and their specific perspective.
2. When individuals present their conclusion and its rationale to others, they engage in cognitive rehearsal, deepening their understanding of their position, and discover higher-level reasoning strategies.
3. Individuals are confronted by other people with different conclusions based on other people's information, experiences, and perspectives.
4. Individuals become uncertain as to the correctness of their views. A state of conceptual conflict or disequilibrium is aroused.
5. Uncertainty, conceptual conflict, and disequilibrium motivates an active search for more information, new experiences, and a more adequate cognitive perspective and reasoning process in hopes of resolving the uncertainty . . .
6. By adapting their cognitive perspective and reasoning through understanding and accommodating the perspective and reasoning of others, a new reconceptualized, and reorganized conclusion is derived. Novel solutions and decisions that, on balance, are qualitatively better are detected.

When we forgo challenging others, we reduce their learning and ours.

Confirm Others' Personal Competence When Disagreeing With Their Ideas

When we challenge a colleague's reasoning or data we hope they will respond with insight and appreciation. It is sometimes the case that even with our repeated attempts to 'make them understand' our colleague does not change his or her view. We are then likely to experience dissonance ourselves. How is it that our colleague could fail to see what is so obvious to us? We find ourselves with only two ways we can get ourselves out of the dilemma we have created, neither of which is comfortable. We can reconsider whether our own view might be wrong, or we can assume that our colleague is just not smart (open, experienced, honest) enough to see what is so obvious to us. It is the latter choice that causes us to attack our colleague's competence, although we often do it with the subtleness of language and tone. This dichotomous thinking into which we place ourselves leaves us needing to place blame, or wrongness, on one side or the other. One way out of this dilemma is perspective taking.

Voice the Perspective of Others

Voicing perspective is the act of paraphrasing the ideas and arguments of others. Perspective taking is more than just being able to play back others' arguments in order to check with them for accuracy. It is the ability to comprehend and voice how the situation appears from another's perspective. Perspective taking is the opposite of egocentrism, in which the individual is locked into a single view of the situation and is unaware of the limitations of that view or that other viable perspectives may exist.

When one voices the perspective of another, that action inclines the other to disclose information more fully than if the perspective was not voiced. The additional information and the fuller comprehension of another perspective both work to increase the development of new knowledge out of varying perspectives on a complex issue. However, it is necessary to hold both one's own and others' perspectives in mind at the same time to develop new knowledge. Simply listening to another's perspective is less facilitative of the creation of new knowledge than is the actual voicing of the other's perspective. We place such a high value on information that it is almost counter-intuitive to realize that the amount of actual information within a group is less important in reaching a high-quality solution to a problem than is actually voicing others' perspectives.

Make the Reasoning that Supports One's Own Position Explicit

We are inclined to be parsimonious in our talk. We do not want to bore others or be accused of saying to them what they already know. So we often talk in shorthand; we state our conclusions but not our data. We speak at a high level of abstraction and leave out the examples that would illustrate our meaning. We make declarative statements in a way that indicates to others that the statements are self-evident; we say 'That just will not work!'. Ambrose Bierce defined 'self-evident' as evident to oneself and to nobody else.

But, as we saw in Chapter 2, each of us makes very different interpretations of the information we receive. We construct very different meanings for terms like honesty, integrity, empowerment and responsibility. To make our meaning clear to others or to make use of others to correct our meaning, we have to offer our reasoning as well as our conclusions. We have to say not only what we think, but why we think that. In so doing we give others the opportunity to determine for themselves whether the data warrants the conclusion.

Although the cognitive benefits to the receiver of such an exchange are apparent, there is evidence that it is the speaker who makes the greatest cognitive gains from such an exchange. Recent studies have shown that the act of orally summarizing information works to strengthen the speaker's understanding of that information. Such a finding would seem to bear out the insight of the Roman philosopher who said '*Qui docet descit*'. Whoever teaches learns twice. Individuals organize information differently if they are going to present it to others than if they are trying to understand it for their own sake. It is in the act of speaking that we tend to organize cognitively what we know.

Change Position When Others Offer Convincing Data and Rationale

This skill is about being willing to be influenced by the cogent arguments of others: using logical reasoning to determine when the conclusions of others are valid. We sometimes think of changing positions in pejorative terms as 'giving in'. But this skill is not about losing or compromising, it is about making an agreement with others that we will use the capability of our minds to make sense of the information. We will not say something makes sense when it does not, and we will change our position when the data are convincing.

Regard Assertions, Our Own and Others', as Hypotheses to be Tested

This is probably the most difficult of all the skills to implement. It is not so difficult for us to hold others' assertions as hypotheses to be tested, but incredibly difficult for us to hold our own. The way Argyris (1986) suggests that we deal with this difficulty is to ask others for help; that we literally end our statement or conclusion with a request for others to tell us if they see it differently; to ask others to help us see where we may be mistaken.

Bohm (1985) says simply, ideas must be vulnerable. 'We have to have enough faith in our world-view to work from it, but not that much faith that we think it's the final answer' (p. 4).

It is difficult to use the skills I have listed here in the fast-paced, business as usual, environment of most organizations.

To have organizational dialogue it is necessary to establish the time needed. That time does not, of course, need to be time away from work, because the dialogue is about the work. The meetings that Johnsonville Foods had to think through the production capacity were a time set aside for dialogue. There are other ways to deal with the time issue. In some meetings there is an identified time for dialogue and a separate time for discussion.

Changing Tacit Organizational Assumptions

A paradox of organizational learning is that organizations can only learn through their individual members, yet organizations create systemic constraints that prevent their individual members from learning.

Argyris (1990) suggests some familiar organizational practices that limit learning, such as transferring poor employees from one division to another rather than firing them; implementing a programme that the implementors know will not solve the problem; softening bad news that is sent upward; concealing an unattractive programme within an attractive one; selling a programme modestly while concealing its magnitude; and getting the agreement of principal players before a meeting while acting in the meeting as though no such agreement has been reached. These organizational practices are not written down but may, nevertheless, be understood by organizational members as the way to get things done in this organization. They can be explained as organizational theories of action; if you want to accomplish A under circumstances B then do C (see Fig. 5.2). To use one of the examples listed above, if (A) you want to get management support for a programme when (B) you believe support will not be forthcoming, then (C) play down the extent of the programme until it has gained a foothold and then ask for what was really needed.

Defensive routines occur because organizational members feel caught. They want to accomplish certain goals assigned to them by the organization; they have learned that the espoused organizational processes will not allow them to

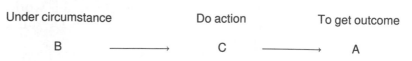

Under circumstance   Do action   To get outcome

B   ⟶   C   ⟶   A

Figure 5.2   Argyris' framework for a theory of action.

accomplish those goals; they believe that they cannot openly address the fact that the espoused processes do not work without embarrassment or threat; they develop a way to accomplish the goals while by-passing the threat; and they develop ways to hide the fact that they have by-passed the threat. Defensive routines become so familiar to organizational members that they become tacit. They are the accepted practice of the organization and have become a part of the collective meaning structures.

There are, however, unintended consequences from such organizational defensive routines. For example, when poorly performing employees are transferred instead of fired, the organization retains a workforce that is inefficient, lowering its productivity and performance. A second and equally serious unintended consequence is that learning is prevented. By circumventing problems, organizational members leave the problem unaddressed. The organization does not learn how to deal with its poor performers because the issue is not openly addressed. Argyris (1990, p. 25) notes:

> Organizational defensive routines are actions or policies that prevent individuals or segments of the organization from experiencing embarrassment or threat. Simultaneously, they prevent people from identifying and getting rid of the causes of the potential embarrassment or threat. Organizational defensive routines are antilearning, overprotective, and self-sealing.

Argyris (1986) suggests that to overcome these defensive routines groups of organizational members should work together to map the causal relationships between organizational goals, actions and outcomes, including the unintended consequences (see Fig. 5.3). These maps can serve as a vehicle for organizational dialogue about the organization's assumptions. Organizational learning does not occur in the making of the map; the learning is the inquiry which alters these

Conditions	Dilemmas and assumptions	Actions	Consequences
Demands and constraints	How organization's members feel caught or what they believe	What organization's members do	Impact on business results, attitudes, relationships

Figure 5.3   Framework for an organizational causal map.

Conditions	Dilemmas and assumptions	Actions	Consequences
Low productivity	Managers who discipline poor performers are viewed as 'not people-oriented'	When employees perform poorly managers transfer employees to other departments	Large numbers of poor performers are retained in the organization
Organization attempting to improve morale by being more people-oriented	Manager's chances of promotion theatened	Managers act as if they are following correct organization procedures	The organization does not learn how to deal with poor performers
Strong pressure to reach performance targets			

Figure 5.4   Organizational causal map – low productivity.

maps in ways that bring the organization's action closer to its espoused theory or perhaps changes both to gain the congruence needed. This public map-making process serves to place the tacit collective meaning structures back into the accessible meaning of the individuals, where it can be challenged, tested and altered.

Conditions	Dilemmas and assumptions	Actions	Consequences
Pressure to keep costs low	Distrust of management's ability to understand the needs of the unit	Prepare initial programme request in a way that camouflages the true costs	Management view programme managers as poor judges of cost
Pressure to provide new services		Ask for adequate funds after organization is committed to the programme	Management tightens budget controls
			No learning about how to budget appropriately

Figure 5.5   Organizational causal map – budget.

The maps demonstrate the systemic nature of organizational problems (see Figs. 5.4 and 5.5). It is often clear from such maps that the cause is not, for example, managers who are acting improperly, but rather that the system prevents managers from acting in ways that the system wishes managers to act. The solution must also be at the system level.

Collective interpretation of information only works if all individuals actively work towards the learning of others as well as themselves. I am not simply implying a situation in which I will learn what I need from the collective and you must make sure you learn what you need as well. I am suggesting that unless others learn, our own learning is lessened. And moreover, I am suggesting that we have a responsibility to work actively towards the learning of others. Like good tennis players who only improve if their competitors are skilled, my thinking is not sufficiently challenged by someone who cannot apprehend the concept I am considering, or someone who knows so little about my world that I soon tire of the long explanation in preface to the issue I wish to discuss.

Knowledge and understanding is one of the few commodities in the world that grows through use. It is not a competition; the more you know the more I can know. If I want to know more I will have to see to it that you know more. That is perhaps, not an easy concept to grasp, schooled as we all were in individual learning, where helping your neighbour learn was called cheating. But that model was from a time in which we thought learning was about taking in a prescribed knowledge, not about 'naming the world'. In organizations we are a community of learners.

Step 4 – Authority to Take Responsible Action Based on the Interpreted Meaning

There is an apocryphal story told about the composer Brahms. He was in a sitting room where someone else was at the piano, idly playing notes and chords. In the middle of playing the pianist abruptly left. After a few moments Brahms got up, went to the piano, and finished the progression. His comment was, 'We cannot let that chord go unresolved forever'. There is, in all of us, a propensity to do what needs doing. That inclination is particularly strong when we are knowledgeable about the issues involved. Brahms's need to resolve the chord progression was acute because he so thoroughly understood what chord should come next in the progression. It was knowledge that pulled him from his chair and into action.

When an organization involves its members in the generation of information and positions that information in the
organizational context, and when members collectively
interpret that information, but the organization stops short of
authorizing organizational members to act on the knowledge
they have derived, the learning is lost. To understand what
needs doing, but to be prevented from acting on that
knowledge leads to anger or despair, or in some situations,
subversion.

So strong is the compulsion to act on what we know that in
many situations we find organizational members going to
great lengths to do what they know needs doing, in spite of
clear instructions to the contrary.

That is not to say that organizational members always do
what needs to be done. They obviously do not. The
circumstance I am referencing relates to action taken when
knowledge is also present; that is, organizational members
have the necessary information and have come to understand
it in their own context. That circumstance is quite different
from when someone in authority says 'you should take a
certain action' or that 'it is your responsibility to do something', without the organizational member necessarily having
knowledge that lends meaning to that action. Under such
circumstances it is often quite difficult to get organizational
members to take action. In fact, we have a term specifically
for that situation: resistance to change.

There were many examples of control at the local level in
the three case examples. The fieldworkers with WHO were
able to change their procedures to take advantage of local
customs. The factory workers at Chaparral not only spontaneously met on the floor to interpret the information
collectively, they also had authority to act on their interpretation.

If organizational members are to act responsibly, then they
must have enough discretion in their actions to make changes
when and where they are needed. Herbst (1974) describes
'minimum critical specification' as specifying 'no more than
is absolutely necessary for a system to begin operation so that
the system can find its own design' (Morgan and Ramirez,
1983, p. 6). Rather than pre-designing as much as possible,
the goal is to pre-design as little as possible. It may, in fact, be
necessary to specify only the negatives; that is, the limits of
action to be avoided rather than the specific actions to be
taken. The story about the development of the Honda City
car is that Honda gave the designers only two instructions,
'come up with a product concept fundamentally different

from anything the company had ever done before, and second, to make a car that was inexpensive but not cheap' (Nonaka, 1991, p. 100). Gore reportedly takes minimum critical specifications so far as to tell new employees to 'go find yourself a job and come back in 60 days'.

The reduction of risk is as necessary to taking responsible action as is having the authority. Chaparral has a no-risk policy. At Wexner, 'buyers are graded not only on their successes, but also on their failures. Too many hits means the buyer isn't taking enough chances' (*Forbes*, 1987).

Finally, in regard to taking responsible action it is important to note the need for a more equitable way to share in the financial gain of the organization. Both Chaparral and Johnsonville Foods have profit-sharing plans. When organizational members have full information about the organization's profit and loss, when they are apprised of the amount of dollar savings their actions have caused, or the increase in earnings their team's new process has made, when they are asked to be responsible for these actions, they will eventually expect to have an equitable share of the rewards.

I have in this section outlined some of the processes and elements organizations have employed to implement each step of the organizational learning cycle. I do not have any sense that I have captured them all nor that the ones I have provided would work well in other organizations. The essence of organizational learning is the organization's ability to use the amazing mental capability of all of its members to create the kind of processes that will improve its own learning capacity.

References

Ackoff, R. L. (1981). *Creating the Corporate Future*. New York: John Wiley & Sons.

Argyris, C. (1986). Skilled incompetence. *Harvard Business Review*, September/October. pp. 74–79.

Argyris, C. (1990). *Overcoming Organizational Defenses*. Boston: Allyn and Bacon.

Bohm, D. (1990). On Dialogue (transcript). Ojai CA: David Bohm Seminars.

Bohm, D. (1985). *Unfolding Meaning*. New York: Routledge & Kegan Paul Inc.

Brooks, A. (1993). Collective team learning in work organizations. *HRD Professors' Network 1993 Conference Proceedings*, Atlanta, Georgia.

Daft, R. L. and Huber, G. P. (1987). How organizations learn: A communication framework. *Research in the Sociology of Organizations*, **5**, 1–36.

Forbes Magazine, (1987), April, p. 26.

Freire, P. (1970). *Pedagogy of the Oppressed*. Harmondsworth: Penguin.

Friedlander, F. (1984). Patterns of individual and organizational learning, in *The Executive Mind*, (ed. S. Srivastva), pp. 192–220. San Francisco: Jossey-Bass.

Hatano, G. and Inagaki, K. (1991). Sharing cognition through collective comprehension activity, in (eds. L. B. Resnick, J. M. Levine, and S. D. Teasley), pp. 331–48. *Socially Shared Cognition* Washington DC: American Psychological Association.

Herbst, P. G. (1974). *Socio-technical Design*. London: Tavistock.

Johnson, D. W. and Johnson, R. T. (1989). *Cooperation and Competition: Theory and Research*. Edina MN: Interaction Book Company.

Morgan, G. and Ramirez, R. (1983). Action learning: A holographic metaphor for guiding social change. *Human Relations*, **37** (1), 1–28.

Nonaka, I. (1991). The knowledge-creating company. *Harvard Business Review*, November/December, 96–104.

Revans, R. (1983). *ABC of Action Learning*. London: Chartwell-Bratt.

Schon, D. A. (1979). Organizational learning, in *Beyond Method: Strategies for Social Research* (ed. G. Morgan), pp. 114–127. Newbury Park CA: Sage.

Tushman, M. L., and Scanlan, T. J. (1981). Boundary spanning individuals: Their role in information transfer and their antecedents. *Academy of Management Journal*, **24** (2), pp. 289–305.

6

Accelerating the
Organizational Learning Cycle

As change accelerates and competition stiffens, organizations need to find ways to speed up the organizational learning cycle; to move more quickly from the generation of information to integration to interpretation and then to action.

A number of organizations have been experimenting with specially designed events that remove organizational members from their 'business as usual' environment and create a special environment in which all four steps of the organizational learning cycle can occur almost simultaneously. These events often involve 60 to 200 people in a meeting that might last anywhere from a few hours to several days. A leader in the development of these accelerated learning events has been General Electric with its Work-Out process and its adaption of Wal-Mart's Quick Market Intelligence. Other such events which organizations have used to accelerate learning are Strategic Search Conferences, Open Space Technology, and many of the large system change efforts. I describe several of these events here.

I should note that none of these events is labelled by organizations as a learning event; rather, their labels reflect their purposes, which typically are the planning or resolution of work-related issues. Learning is the means through which such issues are addressed rather than the goal. The events encompass, however, the steps outlined in the organizational learning cycle.

Work-Out

Work-Out is a process developed at General Electric (GE) to change the organizational culture. Originally devised to rid GE of the unnecessary work that it had accumulated over the years, over time it has changed its character to focus on the broader issues of empowerment and trust building.

A Work-Out session brings together 50 or more people who share a common work process to think together about improving that process. The meetings are facilitated by human resource professionals, who before the sessions begin talk with organizational members to find out what issues need to be addressed. From those findings, management selects key issues and identifies participants to attend the two and a half day town meeting (a democratic forum which everyone is invited to to discuss the issues and make decisions collectively).

Work-Out starts with management acknowledging its commitment to the process. This is typically followed by team-building activities to establish a cooperative tone. Over the next two days participants work as teams on each of the key issues. The teams may use brainstorming, process mapping or a host of other techniques to think through the problems related to the identified issues. Out of this work the teams make recommendations to management about how to resolve the problems. Still within the framework of the two and a half day meeting, management is required either to accept or reject the recommendations made by the teams. If a recommendation is rejected, management must provide an explanation. GE's experience is that over 90 per cent of the recommendations made by the teams are accepted. Once a recommendation is accepted it is again the responsibility of the team who came up with the recommendation to develop and carry out the implementation. Follow-up is scheduled to check on implementation progress.

Through Work-Out it is the workers themselves who find ways to resolve the problems that are identified. Management's role is limited to providing support and to removing barriers that get in the way of the teams working the process. Anyone, at any level, can call for a Work-Out session in their area, although the process does need the agreement of management to move forward. GE sees the major principles of Work-Out as speed, simplicity and self-confidence in action.

Quick Market Intelligence

Quick Market Intelligence (QMI) is a process originated by Wal-Mart, but one that swiftly spread to other companies. It involves rapid cycles of information gathering, interpretation, decision-making and communication. Regional managers spend from Monday to Thursday in the field visiting Wal-Mart and competitor stores. On Friday the regional managers come together in a town meeting, a large group of 80–100 people that includes key buyers, functional heads and

Vice-Presidents, as well as selected representatives of the sales force.

The objectives of the meeting are (1) information sharing of both hard data and anecdotal information and (2) decision-making. The agenda is based on issues identified before the meeting from the field input, but the meeting is open to any actionable issue participants want to raise. Ownership is assigned for all decisions the group makes to someone who can fix it.

The same day the town meeting is held a video broadcast is made to store managers to communicate the new actions that were decided on in the meeting. Wal-Mart reports great success with QMI; for example, opportunities that could only be taken advantage of with immediate response are accepted, mistakes are caught early on, and customized changes for special customers are accomplished.

The major factors that make QMI a success are getting multiple stakeholders in the room, having the people in the room who have the data, involving the stakeholders in the interpretation of the data, immediate decision making and swift communication to those who can implement.

| **Strategic Search Conferences** | Weisbord (1992) has popularized a process for involving the whole organization in the development of strategy, which he calls the 'strategic search conference'. A typical search conference brings together 30–60 people for 2–3 days. Together they engage in a series of tasks that involve exploring the organization's past, present and preferred future. The basic idea is to get all of the stakeholders who are involved in the organization's future in the room together and to have them do the work themselves rather than having an expert or the organization's leadership think for them. The process is basically a democratic one, reminiscent of town meetings. There are no lectures by experts nor vision statements by leadership. The purpose is to learn together about a preferred future and to make that future happen. Each part of the conference has four elements: |

1. to build a database
2. to look at it together
3. to interpret what is found
4. to draw conclusions for action

The conclusions are at three levels: those for individual use, which each individual keeps; those for the functional level, which are reviewed at the meeting by the department personnel; and those that go across functions, which are reviewed at the meeting by the top management group. At each level action plans are drawn up and agreed to, based on the conclusions.

The work of the search conference is done by multiple teams of approximately eight stakeholders, purposely diverse, who conduct a semi-structured dialogue. The intent of the dialogue is not to resolve conflicts, but rather to find 'common ground all can stand on without forcing or compromising' (Weisbord, 1992, p. 7). The search conference seeks 'to hear and appreciate differences, not reconcile them' (p. 7).

There are seven core values which Weisbord (1992, p. 13) reports:

1. The first value is a matter of epistemology. We believe the real world is knowable to ordinary people and their knowledge can be collectively and meaningfully organized. In fact, ordinary people are an extraordinary source of information about the real world.
2. Thus, we believe people can create their own future.
3. People want opportunities to engage their heads and hearts as well as hands. They want to and are able to join the creative processes of organization rather than that being the sole domain of the organization's elite.
4. Egalitarian participation. Everyone is an equal.
5. Given the chance, people are much more likely to cooperate than fight. The consultant's task is to structure opportunities to cooperate.
6. The process should empower people to feel more knowledgeable about and in control of the future.
7. Diversity should be appreciated and valued.

The model described here is based on Weisbord's (1987, 1992) work. Many others have developed models with similar goals, if somewhat different techniques; for example, Ackoff's idealized design sessions (Ackoff, 1981), Lippitt and Schindler-Rainman's collaborative communities (Lippett and Schindler-Rainman, 1980), and Emery's search conferences (Emery, 1989). All are based on the democratic principles of active involvement of stakeholders and a belief that people, working together, can create their preferred future.

Open Space Technology

Open Space Technology is a meeting format developed by Harrison Owen, the purpose of which is to create a space in which breakthrough ideas can emerge. An Open Space conference is held in a large room without much furniture but with a great deal of wall space to put up ideas and notices. The essence of the conference is embedded in the rules Owen (1992) has constructed for it:

- There is no agenda, but there is a theme that is stated at the beginning of the conference
- No one is in charge
- The meeting starts with everyone standing or sitting in a circle where they can see each other
- Each participant who chooses, identifies some issue related to the theme for which he or she is willing to take responsibility. The title is announced and then written on a large sheet of paper and posted for others to sign up. The circle continues until all ideas have been exhausted
- When ideas have been exhausted each participant signs up for the groups they are interested in
- The sponsor of each group convenes the group, leads the discussion and takes notes
- The rule of two feet says that if a participant is bored or has nothing to contribute to a group they should 'honor the group' and walk away.

According to Owen, the lack of form in the process allows ideas to take their own shape, undistorted by status or politics.

Companies that have implemented Open Space Technology report generating innovative new ideas. For example, the US Forest Service convened a 300 person conference to improve their performance. Out of it came a proposal for trading jobs (a Vermont ranger might swap with a ranger in the Arizona desert) that headquarters in Washington put in place. They report that in the 100 year history of the Forest Service, it was the first idea from the field that has ever become policy. Another organization that employs the process several times a year is Albany Ladder, a $25 million distributor of construction equipment. Out of one of their conferences they conceived a new line of scaffolding, and out of another a telephone prospecting programme.

Principles

I have some of the same reservations about relating these accelerated learning events as I had earlier with the case examples. GE's Work-Out process, for example, has been much publicized, leading numerous forward-thinking managers to attempt to replicate the process in their own

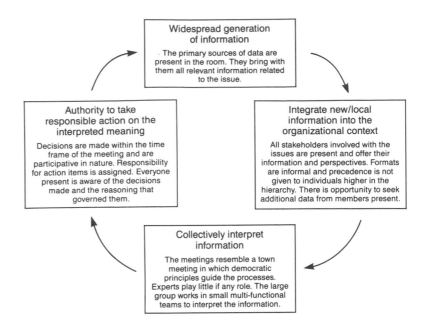

Figure 6.1 The organizational learning cycle related to accelerated learning events.

organization. In some organizations it has worked well, but many, having failed to attain the hoped for results, conclude that Work-Out does not work, or more accurately that it does not work in their organization. And in this I think they are often right: 'not invented here' is often correct. Work-Out was designed to meet the specific goals of GE and is successfully conducted within the framework of its unique culture, it seems reasonable that other goals and other organizational contexts would require very different processes.

My purpose in focusing on these accelerated learning events is not to recommend copying them, but rather to encourage organizational members to invent (another word for learn) ways to accelerate the organizational learning in their own organization. To that end the characteristics of these four accelerated learning events have been extrapolated and related to the organizational learning cycle in Fig. 6.1.

A major benefit of these accelerated learning events is the bringing together all of the individuals who have information related to an issue under consideration. This coming together with information differs markedly from the more traditional situation in which a high-level manager carries second- or third-hand information into a meeting with other high-level managers who also have only reports, not first-hand experience.

Because multiple stakeholders are present at these events the information can be integrated with the information others have to create a comprehensive picture of the issue under consideration. Immediate clarification can be sought for information that is equivocal. The egalitarian nature of the meetings allows information to flow more freely and honestly than it would through the traditional organizational hierarchy. Message delay, routing, summarizing and modification are all lessened.

The presence of multiple perspectives increases the likelihood of a creative and useful interpretation being made and likewise increases everyone's understanding of the reasoning behind the interpretation; if the interpretation is not shared, it is at least more fully understood than through more traditional processes. Many of these events conduct much of their actual work in small groups which meet and then report their conclusions to the larger body. Typically, the small groups are multi-functional and multi-level. In some situations these small group meetings are facilitated or follow structured processes; in others they are more free-form. However, in all there is an expectation of openness and honesty that encourages the challenging of assumptions. The norms of politically correct behaviour and even the defensive routines of the organization may be temporarily suspended. Typically, decisions are made during the time frame of the meetings, often through processes that are considerably more democratic than might occur with 'business as usual'. The rationale that supports decision-making as the prerogative of the higher levels of an organization, i.e. that they have a better sense of the big picture and can therefore make more appropriate decisions, does not hold in this environment, where all of the available information on the issue is made known to everyone present. Thus the meetings are typically more egalitarian.

Although action is not taken within the framework of such accelerated learning events themselves, responsibility is usually assigned for actions, often to those who have direct responsibility for the outcome.

As organizations seek ways to accelerate their organizational learning cycle, I believe we will see many new and inventive events that incorporate these and other principles salient to organizational learning.

References

Ackoff, R. L. (1981). *Creating the Corporate Future*. New York: John Wiley and Sons.

Emery, M. (Ed). (1989). *Participative Design for Participative Democracy*. Centre for Continuing Education. Canberra: Australian National University.

Lippett, H. R. (1980). *Building the Collaborative Community: Mobilizing for Citizen Action*. San Diego: University Associates.

Owen, H. (1992). *Open Space Technology: A User's Guide*. Potomac MD: Abbott Publishing.

Weisbord, M. R. (1992). *Discovering Common Ground*. San Francisco: Berrett-Koehler.

Weisbord, M. R. (1987). *Productive Workplaces: Organizing and Managing for Dignity, Meaning, and Community*. San Francisco: Jossey-Bass.

7   Developing Managers for Organizational Learning*

Traditionally, management development programmes have taken participants away from work to learn from management experts. The experts or their surrogates stand in front of the class, sometimes electronically and sometimes in person, and explain to managers what they need to know in order to be successful and effective.

This way of developing managers is in contradiction to the concepts of organizational learning. Organizations are, on the one hand, encouraging managers to 'think for yourselves', and 'find new answers' while offering management development programmes that provide ready-made answers such as, 'Transformational leadership will solve these problems', 'You need to form self-managed teams', 'Here is the way to resolve conflict'. Management development classrooms are not neutral environments in which only content is learned; managers in classroom situations also learn the lessons of the context. For example, in traditional management development programmes managers learn to trust the solutions of experts rather than their own, to accept rather than question what those in authority say, and to withhold any serious problems they see with what they are learning. This process unintentionally mirrors the very relationship between managers and employees from which organizations are attempting to extricate themselves through organizational learning; that is, a relationship in which the manager is the one responsible, makes the decisions, has the most knowledge and does the most talking.

To be congruent with the fundamental assumptions of organizational learning, management development programmes would have to change substantially.

* This chapter is adapted from an article first published in *Human Resource Management Review*, **3** (3) (1993) 243–54.

- As learning and work become synonymous learning *would need to come out of the classroom* and into spaces where work is being conducted.
- Learning, which has traditionally meant the comprehension of existing knowledge, would need also to include *creating new knowledge*.
- Learning, which has for so long been regarded as an individual activity, would need to be viewed as a *community* or collective activity.

Before turning to specific changes that need to be made in management development programmes in order to make them congruent with organizational learning, it may be helpful to review how I am using the term 'development'. In Chapter 2 I used Kegan's (1982) definition of development as the 'active process of increasingly organizing the relationship of the self to the environment. The relationship gets better organized by increasing differentiations of the self from the environment and thus by increasing integrations of the environment' (p. 114). In an organizational context the 'environment' includes such things as co-workers, job-related tasks, organizational strategy and top management of the organization. An example of development in this context might be a manager redefining his or her role in relation to subordinates, perhaps moving from the role of supervisor to that of coach, or from boss to team member. In this example, however, development is not the change in behaviour, rather it is the internal reorganization of self in relationship to the subordinates that mediates the supervisor's behaviour.

Learning is differentiated from development, in that learning involves new techniques to function more effectively in an existing framework, whereas development is the movement from one framework to another. One of the consistent miscalculations made in management development programmes is the attempt to teach managers techniques for functioning that are inconsistent with the managers' existing framework. The result of that attempt is that managers often exhibit the new behaviour once or twice in the workplace and then revert to their former behaviour because the new technique 'doesn't work' or 'feels awkward'. This 'transfer problem' is most often blamed on lack of support from the immediate supervisor or on a culture that is at cross purposes with the new learning (Broad and Newstrom, 1992). It is, however, equally likely that the new behaviour does not fit the way that the managers have organized who they are in relationship to their environment.

Learning, then, is about making sense of the world through an existing frame. Development is about a change in the frame itself.

Organizations can and do limit the development of individuals in many ways, for example, by preventing people from taking on challenging tasks, by establishing norms that make objects of people, by expecting individuals to act in ways that do not make sense to them. Likewise, organizations are themselves shaped and influenced by the developmental level of the individuals who comprise them. For example, individuals who see the world as dichotomous cannot create an organization capable of dealing with ambiguity. There is an interaction between the development of individuals and organizations that is both the hope and the difficulty of organizational change. The paradox is that an organization cannot change significantly unless the individuals who live in it themselves make significant change; however, those individuals are limited in their development by the system in which they function.

Four fundamental changes are suggested here that would serve to make management development programmes more congruent with organizational learning. They are:

1. Situating learning in real work
2. Defining a less central role for experts
3. Spaced rather than compressed time frames
4. Learning in community rather than individually

Situating Learning in Real Work

Sanford (1981) says that development occurs primarily in response to the challenges of life. It may be possible for managers to become more proficient at technical skills in a 'time away from work' setting, but development occurs in context. Management development cannot occur in the abstract, away from the issues and challenges of managing the organization, because those challenges provide the data and dissonance upon which the reorganization of self is based; they are the grist of the change. Even the more experiential forms of classroom training, such as case studies or role plays, cannot provide the level of reality that is needed for development. In such hypothetical activities the individual is not compelled to experience the frustration of failing at something he or she truly cares about, nor the deep concern that others will suffer for one's mistakes, nor experience the satisfaction of completion, nor the often overwhelming complexity of decisions. Development occurs when managers attempt to deal with real problems about which they care deeply so that their intellect, beliefs and emotions all are engaged. Revans (1983), the father of action learning, has said 'There can be no learning without action and no (sober and deliberate) action without learning' (p. 54).

However, facing real problems is not sufficient for development to occur. Huxley (1972) said, 'Experience is not what happens to you, it's what you do with what happens to you'. There must also be the *intention* of learning from the experience. Kegan's (1982) definition quoted earlier suggests an *'active process* of increasingly organizing the relationship of the self to the environment'. Action must be accompanied by reflection on action and moreover on the outcomes of those actions. It is through reflection that the reorganization of self is accomplished. Reflection is most effective when it involves others who can provide perspective, that is, a view from outside the manager's current frame.

Situating learning in the workplace does not preclude managers coming together, but it does alter their reason for being together. The purpose is not to learn from an expert, or even to learn from each others' successes, but to reflect together on their own actions.

Defining a Less Central Role for Experts

Many traditional management development programmes incorporate action planning that might appear to satisfy the requirement for real work. In such programmes managers are encouraged to try out the principles they have learned back at their own work site: a 'theory-then-application' model. A reversal of that sequence is suggested here as being more compatible with organizational learning: a 'problem-then-theory+' model. To illustrate this model, assume a manager encounters a difficult problem in the workplace, perhaps a troubled relationship with a superior or frustration that the quality implementation has plateaued. Being apprised of the problem, a management development specialist or peers may be able to identify theory and principles that can inform the manager's understanding of the situation. The sequence, however, is 'problem-then-theory', not 'theory-then-application'.

The reversal is significant in that it echoes the new way organizations are attempting to deal with their problems. We are ending an era in which organizations sought *answers* from experts, whether the expert came in the form of the latest management book, an esteemed conference speaker, a famous consultant or the sacrosanct words of the training manual. Organizational learning is not about seeking answers from experts. It is about collecting valid information from a variety of sources so that the information can be considered in terms of the local context and subjected to the reasoning of the minds of the stakeholders. Within the framework of organizational learning, experts are heard and their opinions considered, but organizational members do not relinquish their responsibility for critically reflecting on the information for themselves. Experts are needed and valued within the framework of organizational learning, but their role is less central to understanding than in the past. We are at the very beginning of an era in organizations in which the resolution of difficult issues is found in the reasoning and learning capability of organizational members.

Theory or expert opinion becomes one input among many that might inform the reasoning of a manager who is dealing with a difficult issue. The 'plus' in the problem-then-theory+ model includes one's peers, who may be able to help the manager examine his or her assumptions related to the problem and thereby see the problem in a new light; data that results from action; customers who provide yet another perspective; and other stakeholders who can lend additional perspective and data to the understanding.

The theory-then-apply model assumes that management development professionals are able to predict what issues managers are going to face and thus are able to supply, in advance, theory that will address those issues. The problem-then-theory+ model asserts that in a changing world it is difficult to predict what issues managers will be facing, but that for most real-world problems there are one or more theoretical frameworks that may be useful as one source of input for thinking through the problem.

Spaced Rather than Compressed Time Frames

Management development programmes have typically been provided within a compressed time format, that is a programme that last three days or two weeks. Compressed schedules facilitate travel and minimize time away from work; they allow managers to 'get it over with' and 'get back to work'. The problem with compressed schedules for management development is that they do not result in development.

Development occurs over time. Time is needed to act, to see the results of one's action, to talk with others, to gain perspective, to review theory that might inform one's thinking, to act again, to reflect again, to let go of old ideas, to try anew. The rhythm of development matches the rhythm of the workplace, where challenges also occur over time; problems are exacerbated, get better, decline in importance, then resurface, are confounded with other issues, and are sometimes resolved through no action of our own. Development occurs through the challenges of real work; thus the schedule of a management development programme must correspond to the schedule of the work world. That means a management development programme may need to be spaced out over six months or a year.

If development is thought of as time away from work then a management development programme that lasts six months or a year is unreasonable. If, however, development is not separate from work but is accomplished through work with programme meetings that are spaced out over that period, then the programme is both more palatable and more effective.

Many traditional management development programmes include a kind of follow-up activity that consists of either bringing participants back together to see what they have accomplished or a phone call or survey to check on their progress. Neither of these activities is in the spirit of spaced learning. With spaced learning periodic meetings are a part of the learning, not a way to determine if learning occurred or to report on its results.

Learning in Community Rather than Individually

Organizational learning requires individuals to think for themselves and to use their own reasoning in the service of the organization. For organizational learning to work, individuals' reasoning must be sound. However, as discussed in Chapter 2, the soundness of individual reasoning is often questionable. The tendency to look for evidence that supports an initial view, to give greater weight to more recent events and to fail to check out the inferences made from incomplete data are a few of the many ways individuals inhibit and limit their own learning.

The way individuals are able to correct for those human tendencies and thereby increase the robustness of their understanding is to test their conclusions against data. When the issues under consideration relate to the physical world, individuals can measure and count to obtain objective data. Unfortunately most of the critical issues managers face are matters of interpretation not fact; for example, what strategy to implement to increase market share, or which person would function most effectively as CEO. In equivocal situations, the validity of ideas must be tested, not by facts, but against the reasoning of others. When individuals lay out their conclusions, their evidence, and their reasoning, others can confirm it or point to the flaws they perceive. Individuals need others to see what they have reasoned incorrectly and what they are themselves blind to. Thus, much of the learning that is critical to organizations requires others to accomplish it – it is learning that necessitates collaboration.

Collaboration involves two factors, confrontation and cooperation. Collaborative learning occurs when conclusions are confronted – but only when that confrontation is in the spirit of increased understanding rather than 'winning'. Collaborative learning is not a perfect solution to the fallacies of human reasoning, but the results are significantly better than individualistic learning efforts designed into most management development programmes.

One explanation for this phenomenon lies in the positive effects of dissonance. When participants in an interaction are confronted by a position which they see as sound, yet realize conflicts with their own position, which they also believe to be sound, they experience cognitive dissonance. In an effort to reduce the dissonance, participants search for additional information to support their position and also seek to understand the opposing position, data and supporting rationale. They use the skills of critical analysis and inductive and deductive reasoning to develop, clarify, expand and elaborate their thinking about the issues being considered. As a result of this reflection participants in the interaction reconstruct their meaning, incorporating new information or reframe the way they view an issue (Johnson and Johnson, 1989, pp. 91–2; Tetlock and Kim, 1987).

Thus far two important reasons for a focus on collective learning have been suggested: the help others can offer in validating equivocal ideas, and the benefit of dissonance for the development of increased understanding. There is yet a third argument for collective learning. When managers develop they move from their existing frame to a new and more differentiated frame. The period of transition that occurs as the manager lets go of his or her current way of organizing the world and constructs a new, more differentiated frame is a time of confusion and loss. The manager must come to recognize that the way he or she has been functioning is inadequate and the normal result is to doubt one's own competence. At the same time managers may experience a new sense of hope and promise for the future, the exhilaration that comes with insight. In such a confusing time individuals need the support of others and the knowledge that others have similar experiences. The community of learners provides an environment that both initiates and supports development.

No Guarantees

Management development is a gamble in two ways. First it is not possible to predict whether a development process will work for every manager. Some managers may not develop even when engaged in the best of programmes. Development is to some extent dependent upon readiness. A manager may have recently been through a period of transition with which he or she is still involved, others may be absorbed in personal issues and cannot afford additional disruption in their lives, still others may be so well satisfied with their situation that little dissonance is generated. Lack of movement does not mean a manager cannot or will not develop, it may only mean that now is not the right time.

The second gamble is that there are no guarantees about the direction in which a manager may develop. Development as the reorganization of the self in relation to the world is unique to each individual. One manager may come to see that he has been putting too much energy into work or has been taken advantage of by the organization. Another individual may come to see that the goals of the organization do not represent her values or that the organization's policies are detrimental to the community. It is not possible to say to managers 'Think critically about these issues but not about certain other issues' or 'Examine your own assumptions to see how you may be part of the problem but do not question the assumptions of the organization'. There is an emancipation component of development. An organization that promotes the development of its managers must be open to its own development.

Illustrations of Management Development Programmes

To facilitate organizational learning, four fundamental changes in the way management development is designed have been suggested: (1) situating learning in real work, (2) defining a less central role for experts, (3) spaced rather than compressed time frames and (4) learning in community rather than individually. Five examples of management development programmes that meet many, if not all four, changes are briefly described.

Northern Telecom: Global Leadership Forum

This programme is designed for Northern Telecom's top 150 managers. Managers participate in the programme in addition to accomplishing their regular jobs, spending up to one third of their time on the programme during the seven month period that the programme lasts.

There are two objectives for the programme:

1. To resolve a pressing business issue.
2. Individual learning, which includes self knowledge, learning about global market issues, and global teamwork.

Each class has 24 managers who are divided into four teams of six people. The teams are made up of individuals from different functional areas. Each team has an executive sponsor at the corporate level. The teams work on problems which have been identified by senior level executives, for example, how to do low-cost production in digital switching, or how to manage human resources on a global basis. It is important that the project selected for the team be one that is outside the team members' area of expertise.

The programme begins with six days in the USA. During this period the teams are formed and participants work on team building as well as receiving considerable feedback from instruments that have been completed by subordinates and peers prior to coming to the programme. During this time the teams also define their plan to gather information on the problem.

During the next months the teams go all over the world to benchmark and collect data. They may also assign their staff to help them as well as negotiating with others to help. At mid-course all the teams come together for four days in Europe. Here the teams review their progress but also participate in seminars on cross cultural issues.

The teams continue working on the project for the next few months. At the end of seven months the teams come together again for two days. The Chairman of Northern Telecom and the Vice-Presidents are present to hear the solutions the teams have developed. Each team has half a day to present. The executive group listens to the presentations and makes a go/no go decision on each.

Executive Education, San Diego State University

Each participant in this University Executive programme has a high-level sponsor in his or her home organization who has identified a project the participant is to work on during the programme. As the focus of the programme is strategy, many of the projects are planning tasks, although some include implementation as well. Participants are each assigned from one to three interns from the university to assist them with their projects.

The programme lasts 14 weeks and includes 10 evenings, with some full days interspersed. Participants meet in teams to help each other with the problems they are addressing. In addition to the team meetings, university faculties make presentations on relevant topics, such as change, finance and human resources. For each topic there are also two CEOs who talk about the concepts the faculty presents in relation to their own organization.

Volvo Truck Management (VTM) Programme

The expected results of the VTM programme are:

- Expanded self-insight and leadership development.
- Solutions to several company-wide problems.
- An evolving corporate culture which is better able to meet the emerging business opportunities of the ever-changing world.

The VTM programme is 25 days in length spread over an eight-month period. The programme is held in four different countries, for one week every two months. Twenty-five participants are selected from different divisions and countries to represent the multinational and multicultural character of Volvo Truck. Participants are nominated by the management teams in the different divisions.

Headquarters and different divisions propose projects with the final selection of projects being made by the programme Advisory Board. Criteria for selection of the projects include that a project must

- be a global project that has regional implications
- be of strategic importance
- offer possibilities for risk taking
- have a quantifiable payoff
- be at a general management level

In the programme, participants work in teams of five on problems which fall in areas outside of their present functional responsibilities. Each team analyses its problem and may re-define it if necessary in order to come up with workable solutions that will satisfy the Project Host, the person who owns the problem.

During the week-long residencies about half of the time is reserved for project work and the other half for seminars. Experts both from inside and outside Volvo serve as seminar leaders. A facilitator is assigned to each team to help the group work together as a team, to ensure that both the individuals and the team as a whole learns, and that the Project Hosts' needs are met.

The programme results not only meet the stated goals, but the programme launches a dialogue between participants and top management about the strategic issues of Volvo Truck.

Center for Creative Leadership: LeaderLab®

The goal of LeaderLab® is to help participants take more effective action in leadership situations. Participants must be nominated to participate and are selected with an eye for having diversity in the class.

As pre-work to the programme, participants complete numerous self-assessment and 360° feedback instruments as well as completing an audit of their current work situation. To explain, 360° feedback occurs when peers, subordinates and the participant's boss all respond to questionnaires about the participant's behaviour. Prior to attending the first meeting, each participant is contacted by a Process Advisor who will serve as his or her personal coach over the six months of the programme.

The programme begins with six days at the Center for Creative Leadership, during which participants receive personalized feedback on the instrumentation, develop strategies for effective action and set goals for themselves to be carried out in their back-home setting. Participants in the programme have change partners in the class with whom they process what they are learning from lectures and a number of non-traditional learning activities. Each participant keeps a learning journal which is used for reflection and to communicate with Process Advisors. Participants are asked to set up change partners in their home work site as well.

After their initial six days, participants return to their work for three months during which time they carry out the plan they have developed for taking more effective leadership action. Their Process Advisor talks with them monthly about how they are achieving the goals they have set.

After three months, participants return to the Center for four days, during which they debrief the three months of implementation and reassess their goals and strategies. During this time they again work with their Process Advisor and change partners.

Again participants return to their work to continue the implementation of their plan, often reworked over the four days at the Center. The programme ends after six months with an in-depth written summary of the experience and closure with the process advisor.

It is always a challenge for organizations to create congruence between new ways of thinking and the organization's support systems such as training, performance management, rewards and recognition, and selection. In this chapter I have focused on one aspect of training – management development. It is a particularly critical area, because in most organizations it is the mechanism through which the new behaviours are learned. If management development sends a mixed message about the new ways of thinking, it is not only confusing, it works against the change.

References

Broad, M. and Newstrom, J. (1992). *Transfer of Training: Action-Packed Strategies to Ensure High Payoff From Training Investment.* Reading MA: Addison-Wesley.

Huxley, A. (1972). Visionary experience, in *The Highest State of Consciousness* (J. White, ed.). New York: Archer.

Johnson, D. W. and Johnson, R. T. (1989). *Cooperation and Competition: Theory and Research.* Edina MN: Interaction Book Company.

Kegan, R. (1982). *The Evolving Self.* Cambridge MA: Harvard University Press.

Revans, R. W. (1980). *Action Learning: New Techniques for Management.* London: Blond & Briggs.

Sanford, N. (1981). Notes toward a theory of personality development at 80, in *In Wisdom and Old Age* (ed. J. R. Starde). Berkeley, CA: Ross Books.

Tetlock, P. E. and Kim, J. I. (1987). Accountability and judgment processes in a personality prediction task. *Journal of Personal and Social Psychology,* **57**, 700–9.

Defining a Culture That Supports Learning

Organizational culture is the set of collective meaning structures that organizational members use to interpret the nature of their world and themselves in relation to it. They are assumptions that are so fundamental that they are for the most part tacit. They are not questioned unless attention is drawn to them by circumstances which shake 'what we thought we knew' or by 'externals' whose taken-for-granted assumptions so differ from the organization's that the organization's assumptions are noteworthy to the 'externals'.

That all members hold collective meaning structures in common implies that they are learned. There are at least two sources from which these assumptions are learned. One is the larger culture in which the organization is embedded, that is the industry, nation or hemisphere. For example, Bellah *et al.* (1985) have researched the way that individualism, which has been a basic assumption in the USA since its colonial days, has affected its culture; individualism is a cornerstone of the US legal system, personal relationships, schooling, and even religious practices. People learn their assumptions about individualism through their daily interaction with others who are a part of that society, and having learned the assumptions reinforce them in others through their own actions. Thus individuals are both recipients of and creators of the culture. Individuals bring their assumptions into their organizations, shaping organizations to match the societal assumptions, and individualism is a basic assumption embedded in most US organizations. This assumption is particularly evident when a US organization attempts to initiate a team strategy, only to find that most of its functions, pay, promotion, reporting and training are designed to support individualism rather than teams.

Zuboff (1982, p. 142) provides a time-related illustration of the way societal assumptions may affect an organization.

One day, in the 1860s, the owner of a textile mill in Lowell, Massachusetts posted a new set of work rules. In the morning, all weavers were to enter the plant at the same time, after which the factory gates would be locked until the close of the work day. By today's standards this demand that they arrive at the same time seems benign. Today's workers take for granted both the division of the day into hours of work and nonwork and the notion that everyone should abide by a similar schedule. But in the 1860s the weavers were outraged by the idea that an employer had the right to dictate the hours of labor. They said it was a 'system of slavery,' and went on strike. Eventually, the owner left the factory gates open and withdrew his demands. Several years later, the owner again insisted on collective work hours. As the older form of work organization was disappearing from other plants as well, the weavers could no longer protest.

In addition to widely shared societal basic assumptions, there are cultural assumptions which are learned and held within specific organizations. For example, an organization may be action-oriented, allocating little time for either planning or reflection. The cultural norm is reflected in conversations by phrases such as, 'It's better to do something than nothing' and 'We're not going to get anywhere just setting around talking about it, let's do something'. In a different organization the culture may be more concerned with being 'right' than with acting. The conversation reflects this: 'Let's take our time to think this through'; 'Don't go off half-cocked'. To some extent people are likely to self-select themselves into an organization that is compatible with their own assumptions; but there is also a great deal of cultural learning that occurs after a new member has joined an organization. Some of that learning is deliberate, being offered through orientation or other training programmes, but most of it occurs through the daily interactions the new member has with others who hold such assumptions tacit. Much of the organization's culture is learned gradually, over-time, and without the conscious intent of either the new or existing members.

Schein (1992) identifies three levels of organizational culture. He places assumptions at the base, regarding them as having the greatest impact on the organization and at the same time being the most difficult to decipher. Espoused values are the middle level. Values may be explicated in mission statements or policy documents, or may simply be evident in the conversation of organizational members, as in the quotes above. But, as Argyris *et al.* (1985) have argued so effectively, the values the organization espouses may in fact be in contradiction to its basic assumptions. Therefore, it is not possible to discern an organization's culture from an examination of its values.

The most visible and explicit parts of a culture are the artefacts (the top layer), which are such things as the architecture, the way space is allocated in the parking lot, the way organizational members dress and how they address each other. These and hundreds of other artefacts are observable, yet as Schein notes, are often misinterpreted in the absence of an understanding of the organization's basic assumptions. One difficulty in using the artefacts as indicators of culture lies in the fact that any interpretation of artefacts is made through the lens of the interpreter's own assumptions. A second difficulty is the multiple meanings any one artefact may have. For example, organizational members may dress formally because they maintain a formal relationship with each other or because they are responding to the expectations of their clients who are themselves formal. Schein holds that if an organizational culture is to be understood, the investigation must go beyond artefacts and espoused values and must examine the organization's basic assumptions.

There six general areas of assumptions that Schein suggests examining to understand an organization's culture. They are:

1. *The nature of reality and truth*: How we can know if something is true or real? Is truth discovered empirically, through experience, or reached by agreement?

2. *The nature of time*: What is most important the past, the present, or the future? Is time linear or circular? Do events develop over time, as in the development of an infant, or do we alter and control events to fit our time demands?

3. *The nature of space*: Is space shared or owned as in private property? What is the relationship of space to intimacy?

4. *The nature of human nature*: Are humans malleable or genetically fixed? Are individuals, by nature, self motivated and curious or lazy and passive?

5. *The nature of human activity*: Are human beings a part of the environment or controllers and users of it?

6. *The nature of human relationships*: What level of responsibility do individuals have for others? Are human beings basically individualistic or group oriented? Are they competitive or cooperative? What is the proper role of authority in the lives of individuals? On what is authority based, law, morality, consensus?

The basic assumptions an organization embraces have an

impact on every aspect of its functioning, the way it is structured, the goals it chooses, the strategies it employs to reach those goals, and certainly how it approaches learning. Some assumptions simply result in differing approaches to learning, while others have a fundamental impact on how well the organization is able to learn. In this section I have constructed a continuum for eight categories of assumptions in which I have placed the view most conducive to organizational learning on the right and the view which, from my perspective, is less favourable, on the left. For each end of the continuum I have described the learning approach that corresponds to that view. I have addressed, in this section, those suggested by Schein which seem most related to learning and have added two that Schein does not consider.

Many of the assumptions I outline here were introduced earlier in other forms. I repeat them here in brief to place them within the context of organizational culture.

The Nature of Reality and Truth

The assumptions that serve as poles of this continuum (see Fig. 8.1) are the social construction of reality on the right and empiricism on the left. Traditionally, Western society has embraced the empirical view: that truth can be discovered and verified. Empiricism carries with it an enthusiastic belief in science and the principal product of science, empirically determined knowledge. Empiricism has dominated both the scientific view of the Western world and the lay view of what is true. We ask each other, 'Can you prove that?' and 'What data do you have?' Gradually, however, the newer research in many disciplines, such as physics, psychology, linguistics, sociology and recently cognition, is based in the social construction of reality. Or perhaps more accurately, empirically determined knowledge is understood by these disciplines as accurate within a given set of parameters which are themselves not verifiable by empirical means; that is, they are socially constructed.

The learning task related to empirical knowing (the left end of the continuum) is to discover the 'correct answer' and then to teach (communicate, influence) that answer to organizational members so that they can act accordingly. Empiricism necessitates the reduction of the whole into testable parts, leading to increased specialization. When organizations are firmly rooted in empiricism they see it as more important that certain specialized individuals learn the correct answer than that they collectively understand. The collective needs to know what to do but not necessarily why a certain course

The nature of reality and truth

Assumptions		Empirical knowing	Social construction of reality
Learning mode		Identify and learn from experts who have answers	Collectively create meaning

The nature of time

Assumptions	Learn then act	Act then learn	Learn through acting
Learning mode	Apply known principles	Reflect on actions and the consequences of those actions to derive principles	Design action so that it is possible to learn through the action

The nature of human nature

Assumptions		Theory X	Theory Y
Learning mode		Behaviour modification Reward and punishment	Development of new knowledge

The nature of human relationships

Assumptions		Individualism	Community
Learning mode		Improvement in the performance of each organizational member	Improvement in systemic processes

The relationship of the organization to the environment

Assumptions	Passive Recipient Victim	Exploiter Controller User	Symbiotic Enactment
Learning mode	Adaptive learning	Proactive learning	Co-construction of meaning

Information and communication

Assumptions		Systems structural	Interpretive
Learning mode		Accurate and widely distributed messages	Reduction in equivocality

Uniformity vs. diversity

Assumptions		Uniformity	Diversity
Learning mode		Wide acceptance or correct answers	Development of new knowledge; overcoming tacit assumptions

Nature of causality

Assumptions		Linear	Systemic
Learning mode		Scientific method Experimental design	Action research Naturalistic inquiry Action science
		Single loop learning	Double loop learning

Figure 8.1   Organizational assumptions that facilitate organizational learning.

has been chosen. The 'expert', whether external or internal, has significant influence in such organizations. This view is supportive of individual learning, but less so of collective learning.

At the other end of the continuum is the social construction of reality, a view that the reader will recognize as having been explicated throughout this book. It is built on the assumption that all knowledge is an interpretation, and is influenced by the cultural frame in which it is embedded. Further, all such interpretations are hypotheses to be continually tested and altered. The organizational learning task related to this assumption is the collective construction of meaning. Within this view learning would involve everyone, not just specialists, and it would be ongoing, since meaning structures are continually altered. As Schein (1992, p. 366) notes in speaking to this set of assumptions, 'What must be avoided in the learning culture is the automatic assumption that wisdom and truth reside in any one source or method' (p. 366). The learning task is larger and more inclusive when the assumption is the social construction of reality.

The Nature of Time

There are three sequences of learning related to time: (1) learn then act, (2) act then learn, and (3) act through learning. All three sequences are useful to organizations; however, it is the third that I have placed on the right on the continuum as most representative of organizational learning.

The 'Learn then act' model is the most familiar. When we think about organizational action we typically think about a sequence that involves first figuring out the correct way to proceed and then carrying out that solution. It is reminiscent of the school model where we learn first and then in our later years act. The actor's task, whether the actor is an individual member of an organization or a sub-unit of the organization, is to recall or find the correct principles or processes and then apply those to the situation. An example of this sequence might be an organization preparing to implement a quality effort which, before the effort begins, provides quality training courses for employees, or sends employees to visit other organizations which are successfully implementing quality programmes.

This is an effective model when two conditions exist: (1) there is a known answer and (2) the environment is relatively stable – that is, the environment in which the answer is applied is not greatly different from the one in which the knowledge was developed.

The 'Act then learn' model emphasizes reflection. It is a post-mortem approach in which those who have been involved in an action or project take the time to analyse systematically what has been learned from the experience. The questions organizational members ask themselves are 'What did we learn from doing that?' and 'How could we do it better next time?'. The goal is to derive principles or 'lessons learned' that can be used in a similar situation either by the same group or another part of the organization. The conditions under which the 'Act then learn' model is effective are when (1) there are no known answers and (2) the environment is relatively stable and homogeneous so that the principles that are learned in one situation might be useful in another. The 'Act then learn' model is sometimes applied as an afterthought when it is discovered that, although the actors believed they had the right answer, it turned out to be wrong, and they need to know what went wrong so that they will not make the same mistake again. This model presents a considerable distribution challenge: that is, how one part of the organization can share the lessons learned with another.

The third model is 'Act through learning', but it might just as accurately be labelled learn through acting. This is the integration of learning and acting rather than the separation suggested in the first two models. It may be difficult to think of learning and acting as concurrent because we are so used to thinking of learning as time out from action or even as an interference with action.

The learning tasks are those of self-correction, the invention of new knowledge and the creation of meaning. The question organizational members ask themselves is 'How can we design a way to learn in the process of carrying out this task?'. The conditions under which 'Act through learning' is effective are when (1) the answer is unknown and (2) the environment is unstable and heterogeneous, so that every situation is unique. There is no time for the distribution of what has been learned in a fast-paced environment, so learning and acting must be concurrent and those who need the understanding derived from the learning must be involved in the action/learning rather than waiting for distribution.

All three models of the relationship between learning and acting are useful, though each is most effective under the conditions ascribed to it. The conditions of the integrated model are those that are most congruent with the factors I have described as precipitating a new focus on organizational learning, that is, the organization is dealing with large amounts of equivocal information in an environment that is constantly changing, which gives rise to problems that the organization has never before addressed. Under such circumstances, rather than using known answers to solve problems, the organization must learn its way out of the problems its faces.

'Act through learning' requires that organizational members frame their interaction with the situation through a learning perspective. They start from a framework, which may be a best guess, and then, to use Schon's (1983) words, have a 'reflective conversation with the situation'. They attend to the result of the initial action, for example, how the action has altered the situation, or what other factors are now present. The altered situation may suggest a new action, one not even considered earlier. In fact, the organizational members may never have intended to go far down the first path, but only constructed an experiment to see what information the situation would yield as a result of the action. Schon says that to learn, organizational members must remain open to the situation's 'back talk'.

'Act through learning' requires up-front planning, but the planning is of a different nature from that needed for 'Learn then act'. In the latter, each step may be specified and sequenced in advance, and if necessary could be displayed in a graph or PERT chart. In the former, organizational members must plan carefully to determine what information would best inform their actions and how they might probe to call it forth. Thus in the latter the planning is for what organizational members should do and in the former for what they should learn. Ackoff (1981, p. 205) says, 'organizational learning occurs in response to immediate problems, imbalance, and difficulties more than it does in response to deliberate planning'. It is the intraorganizational conflicts and tension created by these immediate problems that lead to organizational learning.

The 'Learn then act' model is so pervasive, however, that even when answers are not known an organization may attempt to apply it. For example, the organization may demand detailed plans and specifics about cost and time lines in situations where no answer is apparent. When that happens an organizational member or unit who is charged with the responsibility for acting may feel it is necessary to act as if there were a known answer, even if there is not. Having committed to such a course the actor may then feel a need to hide any problems that arise if that answer does not work because not succeeding may be taken as evidence that the actor did not 'get it right' and that the organization needs to find someone who understands the situation better. The 'Learn then act' model allows greater management control than does either of the other two models, and for that reason may be more comfortable to management, who know they will themselves ultimately be held accountable.

The Nature of Human Nature

This set of assumptions concerns the basic nature of human beings. Are human beings by nature passive and self-seeking or inquisitive and intent upon doing the best job they can? This is the assumption set explicated by McGregor (1960) as Theory X and Theory Y. After thirty years it would be hard to find a manager who would espouse Theory X, but less difficult to find managers whose behaviour belies their espousal of Theory Y. The problem managers have with achieving congruence on this issue illustrates how difficult it is for both individuals and organizations to alter their basic assumptions – even when they fully comprehend the benefits of doing so and are making a concerted effort to act in new ways.

If Theory X assumptions are made about human nature, then the most useful form of learning is that which is based on conditioning or behaviour modification. In such situations one group determines what it is necessary for another group to know. The learning issues are how to 'get' others to accept the sanctioned view and to carry out the sanctioned instructions. This view of learning was probably best expounded by Taylor (1915), who said:

> Hardly a competent workman can be found who does not devote a considerable amount of time to studying just how slowly he can work and still convince his employer that he is going at a good pace. Under our system a worker is told just what he is to do and how he is to do it. Any improvement he makes upon the orders given to him is fatal to his success.

If, on the other hand, Theory Y is assumed, then the organization would expect its members to continually seek to make meaning of the events and actions that occur; that is, to continually develop new understanding. As we saw in Chapter 2, learning beyond simple conditioning requires the active participation of the learner. Learning is the internal process of making meaning, and is therefore not visible to others. It must then, of necessity, be voluntary and internally motivated if it is to occur at any level beyond simple conditioning.

The Nature of Human Relationships

Human relationships can been seen as either individualistic or orientated toward the community. Kegan (1982) views this duality as the central issue of adult development. Kegan holds that human beings have deep yearnings for both agency and community and can resolve the dichotomy in favour of one over the other only temporarily; whichever side of the issue is in ascendancy, will, in the next stage of development, give way to the other.

Organizations have, however, clearly favoured individualism over community. Reward structures have been based on that assumption, as has the assignment of responsibilities and authority. It is only in the last decade that the more community-oriented concepts of teams and alignment around a vision have gained credence. The recent interest in organizational learning is perhaps also testimony to a new emphasis on community.

I have discussed the learning issues related to this assumption in greater depth in Chapter 7, and so will only summarize them here. If the organization accepts the view of individualism then learning would be conceived as improvement in individual skills and knowledge, and further that improved individual performance leads to improved organizational performance. Management development efforts would be aimed at individuals, even when offered in a class or group setting. Hiring and promotion would focus on competencies of individuals. Research would attempt to identify the characteristics of individuals that lead to organizational success.

The assumption that humans are oriented toward community would result in a focus on the learning of the collective. The questions would be less focused on individual competence and more focused on the collective processes – what happens in what Rummler and Brache (1990) call the 'white spaces' of the organizational chart. Clearly both types of learning are vital to organizations. It is, however, the latter which facilitates organizational learning.

The Relationship of the Organization to the Environment

The term 'environment' generally implies a wide range of forces which influence the organization, for example, technological, economic and social changes, as well as larger systems, such as government, communities and the industry in which the organization is embedded as a sub-system. There are innumerable ways an organization could frame its relationship to the environment: for example, controller of, exploiter of, adaptive to, victim of, symbiotic with, explorer of. Each frame engenders a different stance toward organizational learning.

I place these assumptions about the environment into three broad categories: receptive, pro-active and co-determined. The type of organizational learning each is related to is suggested. The assumptions of the receptive category view the organization as the recipient of environmental forces and whims. The organization is seen as the object of environmental actions. The necessary learning tasks are, first, to be fully aware of what is happening through environmental scanning or other search processes, and, secondly, to make appropriate adaptations in response.

In the middle category the organization learns in order to control the environment or to exploit the opportunities the environment presents. As with the left-most position, this category views the organization as detached from the environment; the environment is an 'object' which can be analysed and understood in order to be controlled or acted upon. The organization is seen as capable of learning but the environment is not – therefore the environment should be acted upon rather than with. Learning processes might include scenario development, extensive market research and influence/negotiation strategies.

The right-most category views organizations as purposeful systems embedded in other purposeful systems (the environment) which are also capable of learning. It assumes a reciprocity between parts of the system in which each part can influence the others, necessitating that all parts of the system comprehend the other parts. It assumes that reality is, to a large extent, created rather than discovered. The learning task then is, jointly with other parts of the environment, to make sense of the total system and, again jointly, to co-create meaning and action based on that meaning. The organization 'enacts' the environment, meaning it is both acted upon and influences the environment.

Although we would expect organizational learning to result from all three categories of assumptions, how the organization plans and conducts its learning differs greatly among the three.

Information and Communication

To frame this set of assumptions I will draw on the work of Daft and Huber (1987) who summarize two prevailing views of information and communication: (1) the systems-structural perspective and (2) the interpretive perspective.

The systems-structural perspective views information as messages and is therefore concerned with amount, frequency and distribution. Information is distributed within organizations for the purposes of deciding what action to take, to relay those decisions, to impart implementation information and to convey progress and results. The focus of learning is the receipt of accurate messages.

The interpretive perspective emphasizes the equivocality of information. This view is well articulated by Weick (1979, p. 148): 'The manager literally wades into the swarm of "events" that surround him and actively tries to unrandomize them and impose some order'. Thus, a given event may be interpreted in numerous different ways by organizational participants. In order for the organization to act the members must come to some agreed understanding of the meaning of the events. From the interpretive perspective, ambiguity precipitates an exchange of views rather than the collection of additional data.

Uniformity Versus Diversity

If learning is about identifying one right answer, then uniform agreement is to be prized. If, however, learning is the construction of meaning, then the more diversity available, the more likely both individuals and the collective are to escape the tacit assumptions that limit their understanding. As we saw in Chapter 3, diversity is essential to the creation of new collective knowledge. But diversity is also essential to developing perspective on existing knowledge.

The Nature of Causality

The poles of this assumption are, on the one hand, that the world can best be explained by the cause and effect relationships that are related to linear thinking and on the other, that the world is complex and non-linear, and supposes multiple causality. The quality movement has made increased use of the linear view to make significant quality gains. Quality efforts are dependent upon the ability to identify cause and thereby to improve effect.

The complexity of the systemic view makes the use of experimental design to prove a cause and effect relationship less useful. If, as system theory suggests, all parts of a system are interrelated, so that to affect one part is to affect all of the others at some level, then the principle of holding all variables constant excepting that which is the subject of the experiment is not possible. The only hope of gaining a systemic view is, as Weisbord (1992) suggests, to get all the parties in the room at once.

Summary

If an organization intends to make maximum use of its learning capability then it is critical that the assumptions it makes about learning facilitate that direction. To do that the tacit assumptions that are a part of the collective meaning structure must again become a part of the accessible meaning structures of the organization so that they may be openly discussed and consciously chosen.

References

Ackoff, R. L. (1981). *Creating the Corporate Future*. New York: John Wiley and Sons.

Argyris, C. Putnam, R. and Smith, D. M. (1985). *Action Science*. San Francisco: Jossey-Bass.

Bellah, R. N., Madsen, R., Sullivan, W., Swidler, A. and Tipton, S. M. (1985). *Habits of the Heart*. Berkeley: University of California Press.

Daft, R. L. and Huber, G. P. (1987). How organizations learn: A communication framework. *Research in the Sociology of Organizations*, **5**, 1–36.

Kegan, R. (1982). *The Evolving Self*. Cambridge MA: Harvard University Press.

Kuhn, T. S. (1970). *The structure of scientific revolutions* (2nd edn). University of Chicago Press.

McGregor, D. (1960). *The Human Side of the Enterprise*. New York: McGraw-Hill.

Rummler, G. A. and Brache, A. P. (1990). *Improving Performance: How to Manage the White Space on the Organization Chart*. San Francisco: Jossey-Bass.

Schein, E. H. (1992). *Organizational culture and leadership* (2nd edn). San Francisco: Jossey-Bass.

Schön, D. (1983). *The Reflective Practitioner*. New York: Basic Books.

Taylor, F. W. (1915). *The Principles of Scientific Management*. New York: Harper & Row.

Weick, K. (1979). *The Social Psychology of Organizing*. New York: Random House.

Weisbord, M. R. (1992). *Discovering Common Ground*. San Francisco: Berrett-Koehler.

Zuboff, S. (1982). New worlds of computer-mediated work. *Harvard Business Review*, September/October. pp. 142–52.

9 Beyond Organizational Learning

I have two observations about what is occurring in organizations related to organizational learning. One is hopeful and the other less so. The hopeful observation is that many organizations are implementing the processes described in this book. There is a general trend towards making information more available, developing the skills needed to challenge and support ideas, addressing tacit assumptions, empowering employees to act, bringing together those who have primary information in order to interpret it, and designing experiments to inform action. Whether organizations are moving in this direction because 'the smart machine' makes it inevitable or because there is a new awareness of the intellectual capability of all employees is less clear. But there seems little doubt that organizations are making better use of the learning capabilities of their members.

The less hopeful observation is that organizations often implement such processes piecemeal. Organizations are attempting to empower employees without also providing full and accurate information; asking organizational members to think critically about their task but not about the organization's assumptions; encouraging organizational members to think for themselves, but at the same time insisting that they implement processes designed by experts – with which they may disagree; asking teams to learn their way out of situations, but making sure they have a detailed plan in place before they begin. Directions often cancel each other out, leaving organizational members frustrated and cynical.

The four major steps I have described for organizational learning support each other. Collective interpretation is ineffective without the diversity of information created through the widespread generation of information; authority to take action is legitimized by the understanding derived through the collective interpretation; and collective interpretation itself is trivial without those who have come to a more useful interpretation being able to act upon it. Each without the others is rendered impotent.

There is, then, a movement towards organizational learning, whose impetus appears to be the information age, and a pull in the other direction that is, perhaps, a concern about the loss of authority that a focus on learning might engender.

The historical trend is, however, with the movement toward organizational learning and the shared authority that comes with it. Botkin *et al.* (1979, p. 29) note: 'there is a near universal demand for increased participation at all levels'. There is a universal aspiration to be a partner in decision making, an unwillingness to accept unduly limited roles, a desire to live life more fully, a claim to influence both local and global decisions that shape individuals' environment and lives, aspirations for equality and refusal to accept marginal positions or subordinated status. Botkin *et al.* are speaking globally, but the impetus is manifest within organizations as well. The industrialized world is committed to democracy. But organizations within those countries are an anachronism, the last hold-out of autocracy. Katz and Kahn (1966, p. 469) point out that 'perhaps the greatest organizational dilemma of our type of bureaucratic structure is the conflict between the democratic expectations of people and their actual share in decision-making'. We see this conflict played out in many current organizations.

Weisbord (1989) provides an insightful historical progression about how we in organizations have attempted to solve our problems. He says that in the 1900s Taylor had experts solve problems for organizations, in the 1950s Lewin had everybody solving their own problems through participative management, in the late 1960s systems thinking influenced experts to focus on improving whole systems, and now we are learning how to get everybody to improve whole systems. Weisbord's process of strategic search conferences is one way to 'get everybody to improve whole systems', as are several other of the processes I have described in Chapter 6. Having everyone involved in improving the whole system is a way to facilitate organizational learning.

I have, through out this book, drawn a link between organizational learning and more democratic forms of organization. It is, I believe, possible to begin to implement organizational learning without a concomitant move toward shared authority, but it is not possible to move far in that direction. As I noted in Chapter 5, if organizational members have information they will want to act upon it. At the heart of learning is self-determination. The celebrated Brazilian educator, Paulo Freire (1970, p. 76), used these words to describe that relationship between learning and action:

> Human existence cannot be silent, nor can it be nourished by false words, but only by true words, with which men transform the world. To exist, humanly, is to *name* the work, to change it. Once named, the world in its turn reappears to the namers as a problem and requires of them a new *naming*. Men are not built in silence, but in word, in work, in action-reflection.
>
> But while to say the true word – work, which is praxis – is to transform the world, saying that word is not the privilege of some few men, but the right of every man. Consequently, no one can say a true word alone – nor can he say it *for* another, in a prescriptive act which robs others of their words.

Slater and Bennis (1990) predict that organizations would move towards more democratic forms. They contend that the movement toward democracy is not 'some vague yearning for human rights but because *under certain conditions* it is a more "efficient" form of social organization. . . . Democracy . . . is the only system that can successfully cope with the changing demands of contemporary civilization. . . . *[D]emocracy becomes a functional necessity whenever a social system is competing for survival under conditions of chronic change'*. (Slater and Bennis, 1990, pp. 168–69.)

Their list of values for democracy within organizations sounds remarkably like the list of conditions of dialogue suggested in Chapter 5 (Slater and Bennis, 1990, p. 168):

1.   Full and free *communication*, regardless of rank and power.
2.   A reliance on *consensus* rather than on coercion or compromise to manage conflict.
3.   The idea that *influence* is based on technical competence and knowledge rather than on the vagaries of personal whims or prerogatives of power.
4.   An atmosphere that permits and even encourages emotional *expression* as well as task-oriented behaviour.
5.   A basically *human* bias, one that accepts the inevitability of conflict between the organization and the individual but is willing to cope with and mediate this conflict on rational grounds.

A number of theorists (Bennis, 1993; Handy, 1992; Drucker, 1992) see federalism, rather than democracy, as the direction in which organizations are moving. Bennis (1993) defines federalism as 'alliances of more or less independent states'

(p. 205). What such a political arrangement provides is the possibility of functioning as a large organization with the related benefits of economies of scale, yet achieving the self-direction that fosters agility and motivation.

Examples of organizations who are or are becoming federations include, in the USA, Benetton, Dayton-Hudson, Johnson & Johnson and Coca-Cola (General Electric, IBM and Ciba-Geigy are moving in that direction); in the UK, Grand Metropolitan and British Petroleum; in France, Accor; and in Japan, Honda. Unilever and Royal Dutch Shell are international companies that have been federations for many years. These organizations are either large internationals which are attempting to find a more viable organizational structure in a federation or small organizations which have come together into a federation, such as Asea Brown Boveri (ABB) made up of 1100 companies, none of which has more than a few hundred people.

Handy offers five principles of federalism:

1. *Subsidiarity*: Subsidiarity means that power is located at the corporation's lowest point. It assumes that power naturally resides at this level and that it can only be relinquished to a central body through a contractual agreement. The centre governs only with the consent of the governed. Moreover, that consent is established within the framework of a constitution which sets the boundaries of power and responsibility.

   Subsidiarity is the opposite of empowerment. Empowerment assumes that, by right, power resides in the corporate office and can therefore be bestowed upon organizational members. One of the reasons empowerment has been so difficult to implement is that it is inherently contradictory. If power is bestowed, it can also be withdrawn and is therefore no power at all; it is at best benevolence, at worst manipulation. A unit or individual has power only if it is their right to keep the power or to give it away.

2. *Interdependence*: Interdependence means that power is spread around, avoiding the risks of a central bureaucracy. Services that are needed by all are located in the territory of one or two. There is a dispersed rather than consolidated centre.

3. *Common law, language, and currency*: A proper federation needs a uniform way of doing business. A common language may mean that everyone can speak English, but in a technological age it also means that everyone is

connected through computer networks. A common currency means a common unit of measure by which success is judged. A common law means a basic set of rules and procedures to which members of the federation have agreed to abide.

4. *Separation of powers*: Handy notes the organizational trend towards separating the functions of management, monitoring and governance, is analogous to the separation of the executive, judicial and legislative functions of a democratic government. Increasingly there are separate roles for chairman and chief executive, two-tier boards, and separate audit committees. This separation of power ensures the organization's responsibility to all stakeholders not just to special interest groups such as the financiers or corporate officers.

5. *Twin citizenship*: Organizational members have two loyalties, one which is to the company and the other which is to the federation. Handy makes the analogy between the states and the Federal government in the USA, noting that citizens view themselves as both Texans and Americans.

These guidelines illustrate the difference between a federation and the more familiar concept of decentralization. With decentralization, power is granted to subordinate units but can also be rescinded by corporate headquarters. By contrast, federations hold a contractual arrangement in which power cannot be unilaterally rescinded. Federations have a constitution-like agreement that ensures the allegiance of the organization to the purpose and mission of the federation. This agreement, however, also ensures each organization the right to pursue its own ends as long as those ends do not threaten the whole. There is, then, a balance of power between the central authority and the units. The centre exists to coordinate, not control.

There is an incongruity in discussing leadership and organizational learning, given that organizational learning is a concept that acts to lessen the conventional power and attributed wisdom of leaders. In fact, organizational learning implies that leaders' ideas should be challenged and tested through the rational thought processes of organizational members, rather than be accepted because of their origination at a higher level of the hierarchy. Organizational learning revives the belief in individual intellectual ability, and in collective wisdom, particularly when the dialogue takes place in an environment in which employees can, without fear or coercion, speak openly about their ideas.

That does not preclude the ideas of leaders from having influence on their subordinates. However, that influence would come from the quality of the ideas they present, not from their position as leaders.

Bennis (1993, p. 211) suggests three things that are required of the central authority of a federation:

1. Faith in the power of people to solve their problems locally.
2. Willingness to forgo the satisfaction of exercising command and control.
3. Understanding that, in complex systems and turbulent times, no one individual or group possesses enough knowledge to do the jobs of everyone else in the organization.

Although these bear little resemblance to a traditional list of leadership competencies, they may be what is needed for leadership in organizations that are trying to learn.

I started this book by referring to organizations as purposeful systems. Purposeful systems are capable of selecting their own objectives and the means for pursuing them. But they are capable of doing so only if they are able to learn. It may be that organizations cannot transform themselves into more democratic forms or organizational learning systems. It may be that such forms must spring anew – or it may be that we have the intellectual capability to learn our way into new forms.

References

Bennis, W. (1993). *An Invented Life: Reflections on Leadership and Change*. Reading MA: Addison-Wesley.

Botkin, J., Elmandjra, M. and Malitza, M. (1979). *No Limits to Learning*. Elmsford NY: Pergamon Press.

Drucker, P. F. (1992). The new society of organizations. *Harvard Business Review*, September/October, 95–104.

Freire, P. (1970). *Pedagogy of the Oppressed*. Harmondsworth: Penguin.

Handy, C. (1992). Balancing corporate power: A new federalist paper. *Harvard Business Review*, November/December, 59–72.

Katz, D. and Kahn, R. L. (1966). *The Social Psychology of Organizations*. New York: Wiley.

Slater, P. and Bennis, G. (1990). Democracy is inevitable. *Harvard Business Review*, **68** (5), 167–76. (This article appeared originally in the *Harvard Business Review*, March/April, 1964.)

Weisbord, M. R. (1989). *Productive Workplaces: Organizing and Managing for Dignity, Meaning, and Community*. San Francisco: Jossey-Bass.

Appendix A: Definitions of Organizational Learning

It may be helpful to contrast the definition of organizational learning that I have used in this book with other definitions in the literature. I have provided eleven definitions here, listed in the reverse order of their year of publication, starting with the definition I have used in this book in order to provide the comparison.

Organizational learning is the intentional use of learning processes at the individual, group and system level to continuously transform the organization in a direction that is increasingly satisfying to its stakeholders (Dixon, 1994).

A learning organization is one that consciously manages its learning processes through an inquiry-driven orientation among all its members. Kim, D. (1992). Systemic Quality Management: Improving the Quality of Doing and Thinking. *Systems Thinker*, **2** (7), 1–4.

A Learning Company is an organization that facilitates the learning of all its members and continuously transforms itself. Pedler, M., Burgoyne, J. and Boydell, T. (1991). *The Learning Company*. New York: McGraw-Hill.

. . . organizations where people continually expand their capacity to create the results they truly desire, where new and expansive patterns of thinking are nurtured, where collective aspiration is set free, and where people are continually learning how to learn together. Senge, P. (1990). *The Fifth Discipline*. New York: Doubleday.

. . . institutional learning, which is the process whereby management teams change their shared mental models of their company, their markets, and their competitors. De Geus, S. P. (1988). Planning as learning. *Harvard Business Review*, March/April, 70–4.

. . . new knowledge is manifested in new structural arrangements, new culture, and new collective action. Normann, R.

(1985). Developing capabilities for organizational learning, in *Organizational Strategy and Change* (eds. J. M. Pennings *et al.*). San Francisco: Jossey-Bass.

Organizational learning means the process of improving actions through better knowledge and understanding. Fiol, C. M. and Lyles, M. A. (1985). Organizational Learning. *Academy of Management Review*, **10** (4) 803–13.

Organizational learning is defined as the process by which knowledge about action outcome relationships between the organization and the environment is developed. Daft, R. L. and Weick, K. E. (1984). Toward a Model of Organizations as Interpretation Systems. *Academy of Management Review*, **9** (2) 284–95.

Learning results from the adaptive and manipulative interactions between an organization and its environments. . . Hedberg, B. (1981). How organizations learn and unlearn, in *Handbook of Organizational Design* (eds. P. Nystrom and W. Starbuck). New York: Oxford University Press.

Organizational learning includes both the processes by which organizations adjust themselves defensively to reality and the processes by which knowledge is used offensively to improve the fits between organizations and their environments. Hedberg, B. (1981). How organizations learn and unlearn, in *Handbook of Organizational Design* (eds. P. Nystrom and W. Starbuck. New York: Oxford University Press.

Organizational learning is a process in which members of an organization detect error or anomaly and correct it by restructuring organizational theory of action, embedding the results of their inquiry in organizational maps and images. Argyris, C. and Schon, D. A. (1978). *Organizational Learning: A Theory of Action Perspective*. Reading MA: Addison-Wesley.

The definitions offer a great variety of possible meanings for the term 'organizational learning'. Some of the more notable differences among the definitions include:

- A focus on the organization's relationship to the external environment versus a more internal focus.
- A focus on adaptation versus a proactive stance of creating a desired future.
- The learning of individuals versus a focus on the learning of larger organizational units, such as the team or total system.
- Management as the major player in organizational learning versus a broader view that includes members at all levels of the organization.

- A focus on taking action versus a focus on the organization's underlying assumptions.

In spite of the variety and confusion engendered by this diversity of meanings, there also appear to be common themes in some if not all of the definitions:

- *The expectation that increased knowledge will improve action.* Many of the definitions imply that there is a causal relationship between the quality of knowledge that employees have and the effectiveness of an organization's actions. Quality of knowledge may relate to *more* information and *more accurate* information, as well as *more widely shared* information.
- *An acknowledgement of the pivotal relationship between the organization and the environment.* Taking an open systems view, many of the definitions reference the environment as the major element about which the organization must learn and to which the organization must adapt or manipulate.
- *The idea of solidarity, as in collective or shared thinking.* Central to several of the definitions is the idea that organization members have in common shared assumptions or understandings. These shared understandings may need to be uncovered, corrected or expanded to facilitate effective organization action.
- *A proactive stance in terms of the organization changing itself.* Many of the definitions imply that through learning, the organization is able to self-correct in response to environmental change or to transform itself in anticipation of a desired future.

Appendix B: Glossary

Accessible meaning structures That part of the individual's cognitive map which he or she makes available to others in the organization.

Actions Verbal or non-verbal responses that are mediated by meaning structures.

Automatic response An individual's response which is based on a tacit meaning structure. The individual does not need to 'think' in order to respond, as in the return of a greeting.

Chunking The mental act of placing data into larger categories in order to relate the larger 'chunks' to each other.

Cognitive map The network of the meaning structures of the individual which constitute what an individual knows or understands.

Collective meaning structures That part of the individual's cognitive map which is held jointly by virtually all members of the organization.

Collective interpretation Interaction among organizational members in order to reduce the equivocality of information.

Data Awareness of sense data or data from instruments, which are extensions of our senses.

Defensive routines Tacit organizational practices that are developed in order to reduce embarrassment, save face, or lessen conflict, but in so doing limit both individual and collective learning.

Dissonance   An experience of internal discomfort resulting from information that conflicts with the individual's existing meaning structures.

Espoused theories   The way we explain our actions to ourselves and others. Espoused theories are frequently in contradiction to our theories-in-use.

Equivocal information   A given event is subject to different interpretations by organizational participants.

Explicit meaning structure   Meaning structure of which the individual is aware, that is, it is in conscious awareness.

Long-term memory   A metaphorical space where the meaning structures composed in working memory are stored and from which they are retrieved.

Meaning structure   The organization of experience that is constructed in working memory and stored in the long-term memory of the individual. There are many names for this concept, among them, schema (Bartlett, F. C. (1932), *Remembering*, Cambridge, UK: Cambridge University Press), and meaning scheme (Mezirow, J. (1991), *Transformative Dimensions of Adult Learning*, San Francisco: Jossey-Bass).

Meta-cognition   An individual's knowledge of his or her own cognitive processes.

Organizational dialogue   Interaction in a collective setting that results in mutual learning upon which the organization can act.

Organizational learning   The intentional use of learning processes at the individual, group and system level to continuously transform the organization in a direction that is increasingly satisfying to its stakeholders.

Private meaning structures
That part of individuals' cognitive map which they choose not to make accessible to others in the organization.

Situated learning
Learning that occurs in the context of work itself, both in terms of the work space and timing.

Spaced learning
Learning that is spaced over months rather than compressed into sequential days.

Tacit meaning structures
Meaning structures that are lost to individuals' conscious awareness through familiarity.

Tacit comprehension activity
The unintentional mental activity of individuals that is outside of their conscious awareness but which nevertheless leads to the formulation or reformulation of meaning structures.

Theories-in-use
Tacit meaning structures, formulated as if–then propositions. Theories-in-use mediate action and are often in contradiction to an individual's espoused theories.

Working memory
A metaphorical space in which the processing of information takes place; where new information is related to the individual's meaning structures from long-term memory.

Index

140